Happy Birthday, Richard
from Grammy 1983.

Rev. Myron Eells, D.D.

Myron Eells and the Puget Sound Indians

by Robert H. Ruby
and John A. Brown

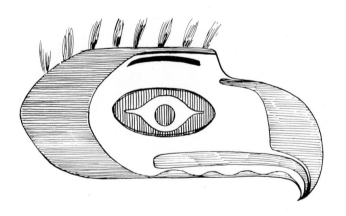

Superior PUBLISHING COMPANY

Library of Congress Card Number 76-2010

Library of Congress Cataloging in Publication Data
Eells, Myron, 1843-1907
    The Indians of Puget Sound.

    Bibliography: P.
    Includes index.
    1. Indians of North America—Puget Sound area.
2. Indians of North America—Washington (State)
I. Title
E78.W3E29   979.7'94'00497   76-2010
ISBN 0-87564-337-X

FIRST EDITION

Printed and bound in Canada

Dedication
To the Ernest Clark family,
and the Lauritz Hansen family

TABLE OF CONTENTS

PREFACE

When we learned through Jean Gulick, former librarian and curator of manuscripts of the Penrose Library of Whitman College, Walla Walla, Washington, that the library held a collection of six volumes of notes and sketches by Myron Eells, missionary to, and student of, the American Indian, we were deeply interested. Our interest in the Eells family developed as a consequence of our preparation of a manuscript on the Spokane Indians among whom Myron's father, Cushing, labored as a missionary for a decade shortly before the mid-nineteenth century. It was at the mission that Myron was born in 1843. Myron's interest in Whitman College, founded by his father, came quite naturally and he served many terms on its board of trustees.

It was from the large collection of Pacific Northwest Americana which the Eells family gave the Whitman College Library that the volumes of notes and drawings are found. Today they rest with other numerous Eells materials in the earthquake, flood, and fireproof vaults of the recently completed (1974) Penrose Library.

In securing access to the Eells volumes and permission to have them published we are greatly indebted to members of the Penrose Library staff. For his kind assistance we especially thank Lawrence Dodd, curator of manuscripts, who answered our many questions, supplied us with relevant materials, and arranged and catalogued photographs of the sketches. We are also indebted to Marilyn Sparks for her assistance, and to Lawrence Paynter whose camera wizardry made it possible to reproduce the Eells sketches made nearly a hundred years ago. For the line copy photos, the greater part of Mr. Paynter's work, he used a high contrast process to produce clear black and white negatives, emphasizing the drawings while deleting extraneous details as poor quality paper etc. Negatives were then washed, dried and carefully opaqued to remove further interfering paper abnormalities. Continuous tone photographs, prints with scale quality, were exposed to plus X film of 135 mm. size using polarized light to deepen dark areas of the rather faded originals. Color photos were made with high speed ektachrome slide film which were converted into small work prints. These were then used to make color photographs. Again, polarized light was used to deepen, but not change significantly the quality of the color. One sketch of arrows on pages 14-15 of this book is from an original thirty inches wide when unfolded out. The reproduction had to be done with special camera which shot the sketch at a distance of fifteen feet after which it was redone in sections.

Eells participated in the World's Columbian Exposition in Chicago in 1893 to help make the public aware of the culture of the American Indians among whom he labored. We trust that our combined efforts through the pages of this manuscript will serve the same purpose in this bicentennial year.

Robert H. Ruby, Moses Lake
John A. Brown, Wenatchee

REV. MYRON EELLS, D.D.

by Lawrence L. Dodd
Whitman College

Myron Eells, youngest son of Cushing and Myra Eells, was born at the Tshimakain Mission, October 7, 1843. In June of 1848 the Eells family left their mission home and moved to the Willamette Valley. In the spring of 1862 Cushing Eells moved his family to Waiilatpu, 7 miles west of Walla Walla, W. T. Here Myron remained for 18 months whereupon he returned to the Willamette Valley and entered Pacific University. In 1866 he graduated from Pacific University, being a member of the second graduation class. He returned to the family home in the Walla Walla Valley where he remained until the fall of 1868. Wanting to study the ministry, he decided to enter Hartford Theological Seminary, Hartford, Conn., the same seminary his father had entered 34 years earlier. On June 15, 1871 he was ordained as a Congregational Minister and his first appointment was at Boise City, Idaho, under the auspices of the Congregational Home Missionary Society. On January 18, 1874 he married Miss Sarah M. Crosby. By May of 1874 he decided to resign his position and search for a more challenging position. Leaving Boise City he traveled to Western Washington for a brief visit with his older brother Edwin, an Indian Agent, residing at Skokomish. During his visit he discovered a need for his services and so the remaining 33 years of his life were spent at Skokomish. During these years he was pastor, at one time or another, for the Congregational Churches at Skokomish, Seabeck, Dungeness, Holly Twana and Mt. Constance. Among this number he organized the churches at Dungeness, Seabeck, Holly and Twana.

Being a very active man his involvement as a Trustee of Tulatin Academy and Pacific University; Trustee of Whitman College; Superintendent of Ethnological Department of the Columbian Exposition for Washington (Chicago); Honorary member of the American Board of Commissioners for foreign Missions; life member of the American home Missionary Society; Honorary member Congress International des Americanistes; member Washington State Philological Society; member Oregon Historical Society; member Oregon Pioneer Association; member Washington State Historical Society; clerk, Congregational Association of Oregon and Washington; associate and corresponding member of the Victoria Institute and voluntary observer for the Weather Bureau, to mention a few, show his wide and varied interests.

In 1890 Whitman College presented Myron Eells with an Honorary Degree of Doctor of Divinity.

Myron Eells wrote extensively on missionary, ethnological and historical subjects. In 1902 he noted that he had published over 1250 articles in newspapers. Such publications as the *American Antiquarian, Whitman College Quarterly, Oregon Native Sons, American Anthropologist,* Smithsonian Institution publications and the *American Missionary* are a few which carried his writings. Along with these items he had published pamphlets and books, such as: *Hymns in Chinook Jargon Language,* 1878; *History of the Congregational Association of Oregon & Washington,* 1881; *Ten Years at Skokomish,* 1886; *Twana, Clallam and Chemakum Indians of Washington Territory,* 1886-1887; *Father Eells,* 1894; *The Foundation of the Whitman Myth,* 1898; *Reply to Prof. E. G. Bourne's "The Whitman Legend",* 1902 and at the time of his death he had completed a manuscript about Dr. Marcus Whitman, which was published in 1909 under the title *Marcus Whitman, Pathfinder and Patriot,* Eells Northwest Collection, Penrose Memorial Library, Whitman College.

Myron Eells' interest and support of the library began in 1882 when he contributed 10 bound volumes, 15 pamphlets and $25. This gift was the beginning of the Whitman College library. His efforts to improve the institution continued and from 1889-1907 he was an active and dedicated member of the Board of Trustees.

Prior to his death, Myron Eells requested that his personal collection of books, pamphlets, manuscripts, letter files, scrapbooks and other historical materials be deposited at Whitman College. Myron Eells died January 4, 1907 and shortly thereafter his request was fullfilled. His collection established the nucleus for an excellent research library on Northwest history. Since receiving this gift the collection has continued to gain in strength and importance. Members of the Eells family, alumni of Whitman College, Friends of the Library and Whitman College all have contributed to the continued support and growth of this fine collection.

1: INTRODUCTION

When Myron Eells went in 1874 to the Skokomish Indian Agency at the upper end of Hood Canal, an arm-like natural appendage of the Strait of Juan de Fuca bordering Washington Territory, he intended staying but a short while. But then, as he later wrote in the objective third person, "Providence seemed to keep him there longer than he first intended." To this agency, under supervision of his brother, Edwin, Eells went as missionary of the Congregationalist Church under what was known as the (Ulysses S.) Grant Peace Policy. After nearly twenty years of service Myron completed his compilation of six volumes of notes dealing with the Indians among whom he lived. He entitled his work *The Indians of Puget Sound*, a region he defined broadly to include the tributary waters of Hood Canal and the Strait of Juan de Fuca. Dedicated to Edwin, it consisted mainly of sketches and handwritten notes interspersed with sections of published notes written by Eells and occasionally others, with occasional handwritten corrections. Although he never published the work, he used information from it in writing numerous articles a number of which were published in leading ethnological journals of his day (see "Suggested Reading, A partial list of Myron Eells' publications."

Unique in the notebooks were the numerous sketches of various items of the natives' material culture which Eells drew to illustrate the written word. These sketches are a focal point of this present manuscript. Although hardly an artist of da Vincian stature, Eells nevertheless exhibited curiosity and attention to detail of the Florentine. His tools were pen, and lead and colored pencil with which he often sketched on ruled paper. He sketched most items to scale, giving their dimensions and other characteristics as materials, colors, and textures. When he did not draw them to scale, he provided original dimensions. Attempting to reproduce them for a present-day publication such as this was a challenge involving the most modern of photographic skills and techniques (see preface). In some of his first volumes of the notebooks Eells relied on the camera rather than on his pen to portray people and places, leaving his pen to portray cultural items which profusely illustrated the remainder of his notes. By sketching these items, however, he was able to clarify their meaning by making his illustrations basic to the thing he wished to portray. His artistic work was basically linear, and his style, realistic. As artist as well as writer, he was basically a recorder.

Unlike the handwritten portion of the notes, many, if not most, of Eells' sketches remained unpublished. Thus, these appear in this present manuscript for the first time. Because of its emphasis on the sketches, this present manuscript comprises slightly less than half the twenty-nine notebook chapters, or, those lending themselves to pictorial presentation. Besides being thus edited, the notebooks have been edited in other ways to retain the pictorial emphasis of the manuscript. Occasionally, sketches from various chapters have been shifted to achieve better balance of picture to chapter pages for editorial purposes. Occasionally notes from various chapters have been integrated in the interest of topical unity and clarity. In a few cases the format of sections of the handwritten portions of the notes has been standardized and the very few misspelled words corrected. In some cases, however, spelling of some proper nouns in the printed segments remains different from that in the handwritten notes: e.g. The religious term, "tamanous," appears in the former, and usually, "tamahnous," in the latter. Liberal inclusions of excerpts from the notes are given in this present manuscript to explain and provide a setting for the sketches and to provide the reader something of their original flavor. Paraphrasing has been kept to a minimum with but few words binding the excerpts together.

In his notebooks Eells exhibited qualities of scholarly integrity and objectivity, a reflection in part on his previous background and training. His father, for instance, had reflected those same qualities in his own writings. After graduation from Pacific University in 1866, Myron graduated from Hartford Theological Seminary five years later. Without formal training in anthropology, a profession then in its infancy, he was surprisingly free of moralisms, cultural shock, and belief in the superiority of the white men's culture which characterized many white observers of the American Indian of his day. He often frankly admitted his inability to interpret as fully as he might have wished, the things about which he wrote, and sketched, contenting himself instead with recording them. This is not to say that he did not effectively pursue his work within the framework of the task he had chosen.

His sources of information were varied. First of all were the Indians with whom he associated. Those with whom he was most closely acquainted belonged to the Skokomish Agency—Twanas of Hood Canal, and Klallams of the Strait of Juan de Fuca. Although the latter peoples in Eells' day remained off the Skokomish Reservation, he often visited them at Jamestown, a mission out-station along the "Straits." Other Indians of whom he showed familiarity were those of Puget Sound proper and of the outer "Straits" and the Pacific Ocean as Makahs and Quinaults in what had become the United States, as well as of several peoples of British Columbia, especially those of Vancouver Island, north across the Strait of Juan de Fuca. Many cultural items he sketched were those produced and traded in a culture complex involving these peoples, and occasionally those south of Puget Sound and east of the Cascade Mountains. (For location of these and other places, see map prepared by the writers.)

He also relied for information on the word of white men who had lived for some time among the Indians. He also depended for information on others who had written about Pacific Northwestern natives, including sketches of these peoples in their published works. One of these was George Gibbs, an ethnologist in the region from 1849 to 1860. Another was James G. Swan, a resident among its natives since the 1850's. Among other sources on which Eells relied were the printed works of early mariners as the Britisher, Captain George Vancouver, and the American, Lieutenant Charles Wilkes, the former having sailed the area in 1792, and the latter, some fifty years later. Eells maintained a wide correspondence with other students of the American Indian, and was a member of the Victoria Institute of Philosophical Society of Great Britain, and a corresponding member of the Anthropological Society of Washington, D.C.

In his notebooks there was no bifurcation between the written word and the illustrations. The two complemented and reinforced each other. As noted, some of their chapters did not lend themselves to pictorial presentation; yet their information was of no less value. Some of these chapters dealt with diverse subjects ranging from measuring and valuing to languages. Others, not tending toward pictorial presentation, dealt with mental characteristics, nomenclature, tabus, and legendry. In one such chapter, "Government and Political Economy," Eells wrote of the village complex and of its institutions as those of marriage, education, government and law. In one of the beginning chapters entitled "Surroundings," he catalogued some fifty species of plants which natives used for food and fiber; and some seventeen species of "beasts" which they used not only for the food derived from them, but for their hair, bone, and feathers. Had the missionary been either a botanist or a zoologist (He did not give botanical and zoological names.) his notebooks might well have been replete with illustrations of the flora and fauna of the region. Nevertheless, in cataloguing with words this floral and faunal richness, he revealed as had other observers of north Pacific Coastal peoples, a natural environment, cool, marine, and aboreous, providing them a generous base from which to produce a wide diversity of the material things he sketched. Interestingly, Eells provided sketches to accompany chapters dealing with religion, usually thought of as a non-material thing, but not entirely so because the natives objectified their religion in material things as images and other items of worship.

A constant theme in the notebooks, and one certainly reflected in the sketches, was that of a people and culture in transition. In the geographical area of Eells' ministry, white contact may be said to have begun with the coming of Vancouver, increasing in intensity, as Eells portrayed it, up to and including the time he lived among the Indians. Less than two decades before his coming on the Skokomish, as he narrated it in an introductory chapter, entitled "History," white men through armed conflict had by 1856 subdued elements of hostile bands of Puget Sound Indians. Living on the western confines of the Sound, those among whom Eells lived, had remained aloof from hostilities. Yet, they did not escape the consequences of the war and the white men's victory, for it insured an increasing white population in the area, with its attendant increasing tempo of acculturation. Indian resistance, as Eells noted, had been precipitated by the intent of the United States government to establish Indians on reservations as arranged for in a series of treaties between them and it immediately prior to the war. White victory had also safeguarded the reservation system.

Eells' handwritten notes, and sketches revealed the process of change among the Indians as both their material and non-material culture shifted from native forms to those which the writer-artist termed "American," sweeping all but a few elderly resisters in its path. He noted, for instance, that the men found employment in white men's occupations as lumbering and milling, and, that even the women, more traditionalist than their men, sold such things as knitted socks to whites and sometimes worked in their homes. Yet, acculturation had not been complete. What Eells termed their "progress" had brought them hybrid-like into a stage of what he termed "half-civilization." In this stage of their "progress," for

instance, they lived in "American" houses whose floors gathered dirt, grease, and saliva to poison the air, and wore soggy "American" shoes and stockings whose dampness produced consumptive ailments amongst them.

Eells' work was in reality a document of cultural change. In this respect, perhaps lies its greatest value. Despite the limited tools (many since available to the modern student) at his disposal, he faithfully recorded a culture in transition. This was not only a tribute to him, but a valuable addition to our store of knowledge. Evidence of his expertise was reflected in his having been selected Superintendent for the State of Washington at the World's Columbian Exposition in Chicago in 1893. There, he showed the world the cultural items he had gathered for that event, some of which he sketched. Now, in their armchairs, readers of this present manuscript have the opportunity of seeing sketches of objects displayed at the Exposition along with his others, many of which have been hidden from view for nearly a hundred years.

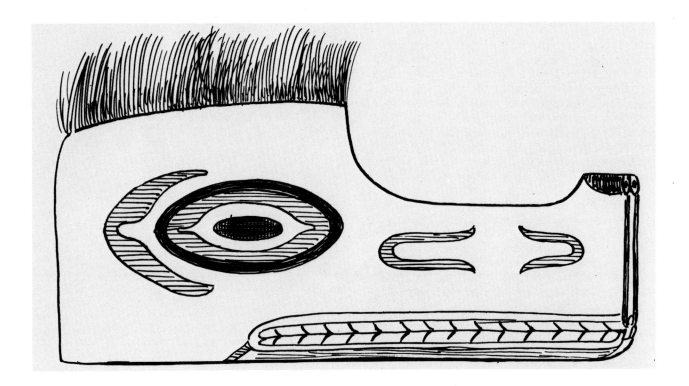

2: SUBSISTENCE

In discussing subsistence Eells described the numerous and varied means the natives used, and the different employments they followed, in gaining their livelihood. His sketches not only catalogued the materials they used in earning their living, but chronicled the changing characteristics of these objects over the years.

Eells noted that for more than thirty years most of the three Twana bands had been gathered on the Skokomish Reservation where Eells resided. Bands of these Twanas, he noted, left the reservation to fish at some of their former places. Klallams subsisted themselves from independent villages, many of them along the "Straits." Some had bought land, laid out a town and built a school, church and jail and gained their livelihood by farming, canoeing, fishing, and working for neighboring whites. At Elwha, where formerly the largest Klallam band lived, they were diminished in numbers. Five or six Klallams had homesteaded land a mile or two back from the beach, "the only ones of the whole tribe who live so far from salt water." These Indians, like the few families around Pysht, lived mainly by fishing and sealing, going in late winter and spring into Makah waters for seals. Eells noted that at Clallam Bay, about 1880, a number had bought some one hundred-fifty acres of land in imitation of their Jamestown brothers, and "raised a little" on their land, fished and hunted seals. "About 1891," wrote Eells, "a boom took place in Clallam Bay, two towns sprang up, the lands of these Indians became very valuable, and they sold out, to dwindle away." Their fellows on the lower "Straits" not only canoed and fished, but worked for neighboring whites in sawmills, traveling to work from villages opposite Port Gamble and Port Discovery.

Eells noted that since Puget Sound natives lived on salt water shores, a large portion of their food had always been obtained from the sea. In his time they continued to fish, but had deferred to the use of white men's gear in that occupation. "They have," wrote the missionary, "adopted most of the methods used by the whites, as the hook and line, and seine, which they purchase, and also make from material they buy." Of their fishing tools and techniques:

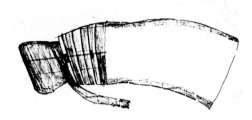

Bait for beaver made from ox horn cut off at the base and filled with beaver grease and plugged with wood stopper and suspended by means of string over an American trap.

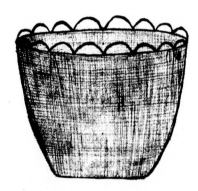

Split cedar limbs were used to make this basket for carrying and storing dry articles.

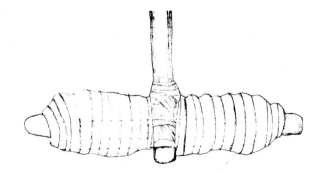

Rake used by Klallams at a Dungeness fish trap to clean off the weir. Handle and crosspiece were made of wood tied with cedar limb rope. It was used to clean leaves, sticks and sometimes, gravel washed onto the weir.

A very common fish spear is made with a long, straight handle, fifteen or twenty feet long, and not far from an inch in diameter. The handle is of fir, on account of its strength, as well as being straight, and the prongs are of some hard wood, as maple, or ironwood, sometimes hardened in the fire, and lately of iron. They are used in spearing skates, crabs, flounders, salmon and the like, and for bringing up cod fish eggs, when they are in water that is not too deep. When thus fishing, one person, sitting in the stern of the canoe, will quietly paddle, while another, sitting or kneeling in the bow, uses the spear. Because of long practice, they will see a fish partly buried in the mud, where an unpracticed eye will fail to discern it, and having seen it will rarely fail to secure it.

Eells observed that as white men entered the fishing business they often hired Klallams to travel far off Makah coasts in schooners at greater distances than they had ventured before in their canoes, to help them hunt seals. Generally in this work

they are employed by white men, who own schooners, on which they take the Indians, with their canoes to the seal fields in the ocean. A few Indians of late years have also obtained such schooners, at least among the Makahs. The Indians with canoes are generally paid a certain share of the skins they catch. Two Indian men go in each canoe, and eight or ten canoes go with each schooner. Other Indians are also taken in the schooners to take care of the pelts. With these schooners they go far out into the ocean, much farther than they did before schooners were used. Generally they live on board the schooners except when at work. On a fine day, when they see the seals, they go to work. One Indian acts as steersman, and the other as spearsman in each canoe.

Of their implements used in sealing:

The heads fit over the ends of the spear handles as with the fish spears, and are also fastened with thongs and lines so that after the head is in the animal, the handle comes out, but the seal is held by a line, attached to the head and held by the person. [Some iron heads were fabricated in blacksmith shops.] The Indian told me that usually he threw two of these spears, one just after the other, but why he did so, and why the heads were of a different shape, I could not learn...

Eells believed the sealing business to have been "very profitable," and that "of late white people are doing a large share of the work in all departments."

In whaling, spears were attached to buoys of inflated fawn and hairseal skins turned inside

Duck-shaped float.

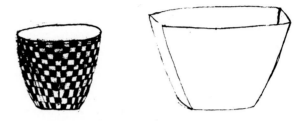

Water-tight baskets made of cedar roots and grass woven and sewed together used for cooking by placing heated stones in water and food in them. Basket with angular rim is only one with such rim which Eells saw.

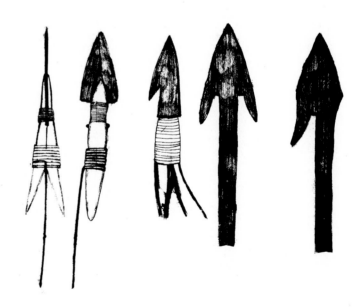

Seal spearheads were made of iron, formerly of bone fastened to long wooden handles. Klallams were only Indians in the area where Eells lived to use these when they hunted seals off Makah coasts.

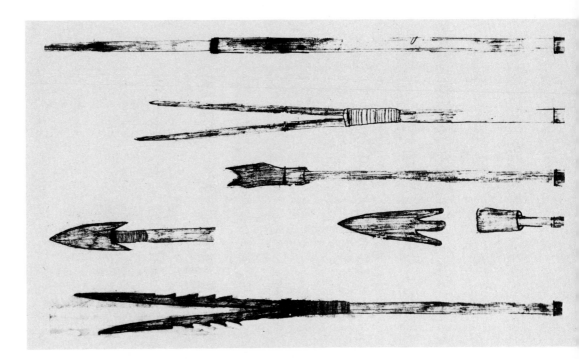

Arrow shafts were made of cedar or ironwood. Points were made of wood, bone, and iron as well as of wire. Next to top is a two-pronged nonserrated bird arrow. Bottom, a two-pronged serrated duck arrow. Top two and the last are of wood. Top one was used in games to see which contestants could shoot greater distances. Third and fourth down with blunt heads were used as play arrows and to knock over squirrels. Two heads to left above last arrow were formerly used in war.

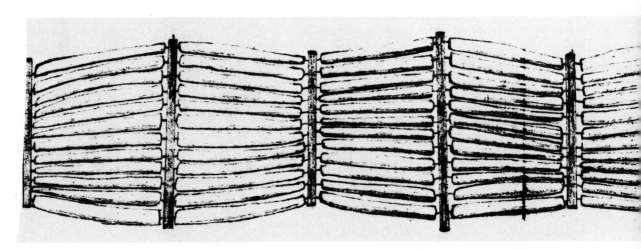

Head band made of dentalia shells.

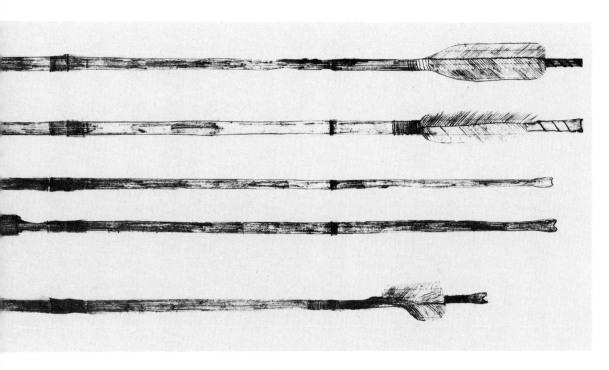

Duck spears. These were made of hardwood, but occasionally of bone and later, of iron usually with three or four notched prongs to catch in the feathers. They fastened to handles 15 to 20 feet long. On left is bone prong found near Port Townsend. Center, one of bone found on Lummi Reservation.

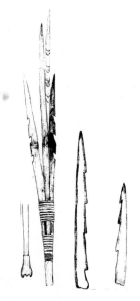

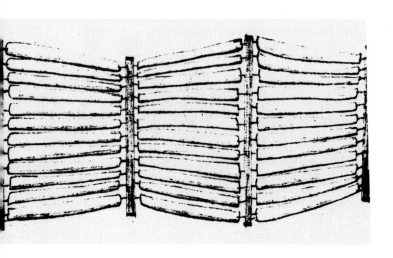

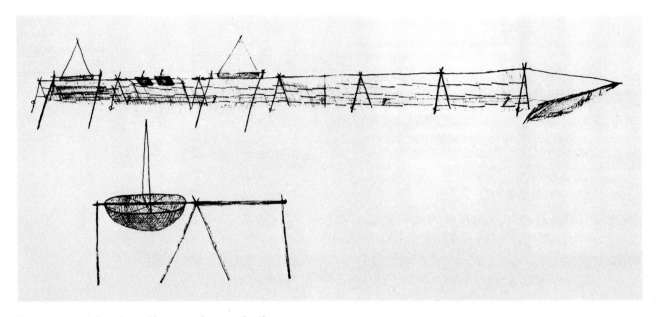

Fire traps like that illustrated were built across streams to take salmon. Also seen is one of the 2-foot nets made of string secured to a rim, 6 feet broad. When Eells was among them, Indians still used string made of nettle or twisted alder bark, although by that time, American twine was mostly used for making nets.

out. Whalers attached fifteen or twenty such buoys to the huge mammals to keep them afloat until they could tow them ashore. "Very little however" he wrote, "is done in this business, as it is too dangerous and whales are too scarce." Indians, he added, not only speared the giant whale, but smaller game as ducks and geese. As he described them, the types of spears used to catch the latter were of three or four notched-prongs spread "so far apart as not to injure the body of the duck, being intended simply to catch in the feathers." Prongs were made of hardwood and occasionally of bone with iron often substituted for these materials. "However," he wrote, "the use of firearms has so frightened the ducks that they can hardly be caught with these spears and they are seldom seen."

Eells observed that formerly natives had used pitchwood torches fastened behind canoes in which one of the hunters paddled and another up front speared birds in the water thus illuminated. Eells wrote: "Many years ago, at times I have seen many lights on the water, of those thus catching ducks and fish when it is very dark, and the scene is quite beautiful." At other times

especially in foggy weather the Indians cover their canoes with green boughs, among which they hide, and they paddle quietly among the ducks, and shoot them. [Formerly they suspended] nets for taking wild fowl that frequent these shores in great numbers. On these poles the nets were set up at night at which time the geese searched the ground for food. Fires were then built which alarmed the birds, and caused them to fly against the nets, by which they were thrown to the ground, where, before they had time to recover themselves, they were caught and killed.

"Cherry, willow and hazel bark," he added, and "the inner bark of the cedar, and some kinds of grass are used without preparation as a thin flat strap to wrap around various articles as fastening heads on to arrows, spears, fish hooks and the like."

To catch salmon in rivers, Eells noted that they built traps across streams: "The weir prevents the fish from ascending the stream. Nets are then provided, about 6 feet broad and 2 feet deep, made of strings and secured to a rim of wood. Native strings of this sort are made of nettle or alder bark twisted, but American twine is now often used." In use also was another style of twine net "about a foot broad, sixteen inches deep, tapering to a point, fastened at the upper edge to a rim of wood or hoop of iron. It is attached to a handle about ten feet long, and is used in gathering sea eggs, and small fish. I have seen it in use more among the Clallams than the other tribes." He noted that string, one-sixteenth to one-eighth-inch in diameter, also used in making nets, was made by hackling and twisting the outer fiber of nettle making a strong line looking much like linen twine. Klallams, he wrote, made fishing lines of the smaller part of kelp roots of about one-eighth-inch in diameter, brittle when dry but tough when soaked in water for some time.

Although Eells knew that common large American seines were used in taking fish in salt water and in the larger streams, he also knew that Indians made large seines of twine like those used by whites by wrapping that material on figure-of-eight-shaped bobbins worked into knotted rectangles over blocks to keep loops of uniform size.

As described and pictured in the notebooks, buoys were usually made of cedar and were very light. Sometimes they were made of large numbers of sticks, ten or twelve inches long tied together to make a bundle about four inches in diameter. Another type was made of a single block with a hole through it by means of which it was attached to the seine. Another type was made of single cedar blocks with handles at one of the ends through which holes were made; another was made in the shape of a duck "especially as a decoy for porpoises"; and yet another, used on whaling spears, was made of skins. Seine sinkers "were of stone, oval, and usually three or three and a half inches long by about two in diameter. Strings of bark are fastened around this stone both lengthwise and crosswise to which the line is affixed. These stones are not manufactured for the purpose, but those of about the right size are selected from beach stones."

The Indians ate or took for their skins twenty-one species of fish and fifteen other marine "animals." They also used shells of the abalone, dentalia, and olivella for dishes, other receptacles, and money. The skin of the dog fish they used for "sandpaper," the oil of that fish, to grease skids in the woods so that logs could slide over them easily.

Where formerly Puget Sound Indian food had consisted "of the spontaneous products of the land and water, as roots, berries, game, fish, and other marine animals," primary foods, had by 1894 changed, for as Eells noted: "The flesh of the deer, elk and bear are dried. They were formerly not so

Made of small sticks tied to end pieces, this frame was for drying salmon and codfish eggs, native luxuries, which were spread on it and then hung above a fire.

Herring and smelt rake and Klallam halibut hook. Fir wood handles, 15 to 20 feet long were fixed with 1½ to 2-inch nails or sharpened strong wire points over 3 feet at one end. This was plunged through schools of fish to impale them. Halibut hooks were made of hemlock roots, steamed and bent with bone point at end of one arm, secured by bark string. Hardwoods were also used for making points. A string was fastened to the other arm.

Codfish hook made of 4 or 5-inch bone point fastened with string of bark to piece of whalebone about 2-feet long. Bait was small fish slipped on end looped for easy fastening and unfastening from a line.

much accustomed to this kind of food as they were to fish, as before the introduction of fire arms it was much more difficult to obtain it." Where firearms had tended to draw Indians from the sea to the hills for game, the camas root, which had once taken them from their seaside haunts to prairies, was seldom dug any more. "These [camas diggers, a tool] have entirely gone out of use on the Sound. In fact I lived here eighteen years before I saw one or even learned of their existence."

Whereas salmon had formerly been dried for winter, they were more and more being salted. "…these [fish], wrote Eells, "salmon, smelt, herring and halibut are dried, as well as eaten fresh. The herring and smelt are dried whole, the salmon after being cut open, and the head and back bone removed, and the halibut, after being cut into strips."

Of the numerous species of birds they captured "It is said that the grouse and mallard were not eaten until the whites came, the former because they fed on snails. None of these were put up for future use, but now ducks are sometimes salted down by the barrel." According to the missionary, salt for curing was not their own innovation: "This was never used until the whites came, and even now they do not use it on much food which whites think they cannot use without it." Eells explained that fish eggs were also dried, and the camas and fern roots, beaten into cakes with fish eggs—all for future use. Because of the abundance of these types of foods as well as several varieties of berries, there was in Eells' thinking "never any need of real suffering…The only suffering to which they almost voluntarily subject themselves is from improvidence."

He noted changes in not only their solid foods, but in their beverages. "I cannot learn," he wrote, "that formerly they had any drink except water, unless occasionally they made a tea of the leaves of the blackberry, cranberry or hemlock. At present they are greatly addicted to the use of tea and coffee. The large share of them as yet use but little milk or butter, for while many of them have cows, they think dairying too much trouble."

Eells summarized changes in the Indians' subsistence patterns:

> The business of the women was to cook, get berries, roots, and sprouts, dig clams, clean the fish, dry the berries, clams, and fish, make the mats, and baskets, spin yarn and make the old fashioned

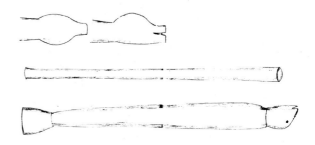

Wooden fish clubs.

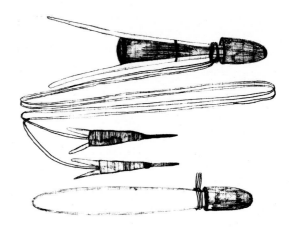

Fish spearheads. Two iron-pointed spearheads, to right of midline, each with two side pieces of wood (Bone was also used.) were wrapped with pitch-covered strings and fastened to pole with thongs. Pole was forked to receive the two hooks. Another part (on left, a side view on right) was made of light cedar wood with two wings of dogwood. This was attached to another pole by thongs. When thrust into water on a pole the wings came free and spun to surface, attracting fish which were speared with the hooks. In this illustration Eells drew thongs of the hooks to the "spinner."

Large fishhook. Iron hooks were fitted to long handles and thongs tied so that when fish were caught, hooks came loose preventing breaking of poles.

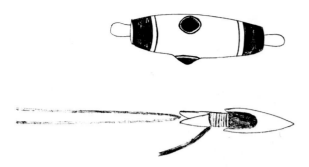

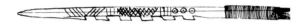

Whaling spear and buoy. Handles for spears were thicker than those for other types of fishing and hunting gear. Joint is of bone. On left is skin buoy fastened to spear when in use.

Example of use natives had for bone—single-pronged duck spear.

Indians of Eells' acquaintance adapted well to their environment securing their livelihood from various elements of it. Their mainstay had been fish. This is a wooden fish spear. Two or three two-foot-long prongs of hardwood as maple or ironwood and later, of iron, were fastened to handles 15 to 20-feet-long and used to spear skates, crabs, flounders and salmon, and for bringing up codfish eggs.

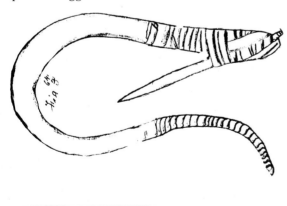

Klallams showed their ingenuity in producing from raw materials about them a halibut with bone point. At left, the bone point.

blankets, and clothes, and some of the ornaments. Since the introduction of white industries, they have been accustomed to do much the same work in the house as the white women. Basket making, mat making, gathering berries, and digging clams, spinning yarn and knitting socks, sewing, washing for whites, and digging potatoes for the whites as well as the general duties of housekeeping are their principal industries now. Socks, washing, berries, and potatoe digging are their principal sources of money revenue.

The men's business was to hunt, fish, make canoes, planks, build houses, and take care of the horses. They still do these things, except making planks. They also do much work at farming. Many of them work in sawmills, and a large number are loggers, preferring this business to farming, even when they have good land, if they can only make it pay. Canoeing for whites has been quite a business with Clallams, until lately. Steamers have ploughed their waters so often and regularly, as to almost entirely destroy the business. Hop-picking in the White river, Puyallup and Duwamish river bottom has for ten or twelve years been a great business for all the Sound Indians in September, as well as for more northern Indians and those east of the Cascades and west of the Olympic mountains. They have made money very fast in the short season of the business. For the last two or three years, white pickers have begun however to crowd greatly on this source of revenue, as the times have grown harder. A dozen years ago they had almost the monopoly of the business, and those who have kept sober, attended to their business, have held their own with the whites to the present times. Many growers prefer them as they are more willing to live out doors, begin early, and complain less than the most whites.

Suggested Reading

Drucker, Philip. *Indians of the Northwest Coast,* New York, 1955.
Goddard, Pliny Earle. *Indians of the Northwest Coast,* New York, 1945.

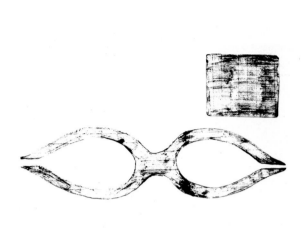

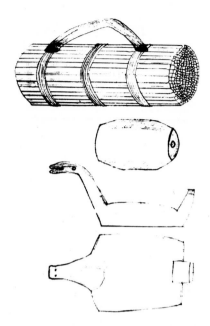

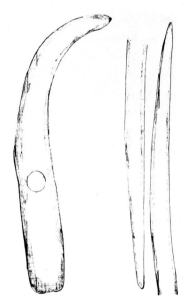

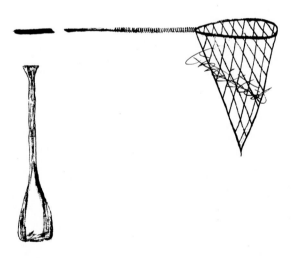

On left, block used in making seines to keep the loops of uniform size. On right, a bobbin for winding twine in making nets. Ends closed enough to make it easy to run implement through the loops when tying knots.

Various types of buoys usually made of cedar. At top is bundle of cedar sticks tied together. In center is single block with hole for attaching to a seine. At bottom are two views of one shaped as a duck and towed behind a canoe as decoy to attract porpoises which were shot when they surfaced to inspect the buoy.

On left is deerhorn handle used on camas digging stick. Such sticks of ironwood hardened by fire were no longer used. On right is two-foot-long fire-hardened stick used for digging clams.

On left a wooden shovel used to dump gravel on bottom of fish trap. On right a net used at end of 10-foot pole to gather fish eggs and small fish. Eells wrote the word "omitted" across the net.

3: BUILDINGS

In this chapter Eells described structures built by the natives. He concerned himself with uses to which the structures were put, as well as with styles, materials and appurtenances. As in his other chapters, he revealed in this one the transition from early structures, especially houses, to those introduced by white men which he called "civilized" buildings.

"Their houses," wrote the missionary, "were originally near the beach in small villages, but arranged with no order. Those at Jamestown are now on one straight street and those on the [Skokomish] reservation are scattered on their farms." He described some eight different house types. The first were potlatch houses, "the only public buildings among the Indians. They are not always built on a uniform plan. One was built on the Skokomish reservation in 1875 which was about forty by two hundred feet...One was built by the Twana Indians about 1868...having been about fifty by three hundred feet. One at Squaxson and one at Port Angeles were also similar, and none of these were used much for dwellings after the potlatches..." In February, 1878 Eells visited a potlatch house at Jamestown. Of this structure he wrote:

The house was built for a large dwelling a year or two before, the potlatch, however, being in contemplation, and was about 32 by 84 feet. It was by no means large enough to hold all the Indians who attended, but in the village there were about a dozen dwellings, in which some of the visitors were received. The beds and seats of this potlatch house were much the same as that of Twanas, but the shelves overhead for storing of articles were differently arranged. Instead of being all around the house over the beds, they were along the side walls, with one shelf across the middle of the house. The two at the ends were used chiefly for storing articles belonging to the visitors, and the central one was for storing food, which included sixty sea-biscuit and a few half barrels of sugar, brought by the guests and presented to their hosts. In one corner a blanket was fastened up, evidently to make a screen for a dressing room.

The second category of house, sweat houses, were very uncommon:

The only ones I have seen were used by the medicine men, but have long since gone out of use. They were three or four feet in height, a little more in diameter, and conoidal. Sticks were driven into the ground in a circle, bent over and fastened together at the upper end, or if long enough, the other end was put into the ground. These were covered with large leaves as maple or evergreen, and the whole was then covered with earth. They were intended for only one person at a time.

Interior view of four sections of a nine section potlatch house. *aaa*, nine-foot-long side support tamanous posts; *bbb*, support posts; *ccc*, bed platforms, two feet above the ground, extending around entire inside wall; *dd*, overhead storage shelf; *e*, panel to the side of each door to deflect cold winds and divide peoples of various localities; *gg*, seats; *ff*, fires; *h*, ridgepole supports; *iii*, large round crossbeams resting on *aaa*, and on which rested posts *bbb*. This particular house had three doors on front side facing the water, one at each end, but none at the back which was against the hill.

The third house type, large dwelling houses, were

usually twenty five or thirty feet wide by thirty, forty or fifty feet long, though occasionally they are nearly twice as long. Each house is owned by one man, but intended for several families, usually his friends and relations, who pay no rent. There is no floor but the ground. The doors are either at each end...or in the middle of one side. There are small walls on each side of the entrance, inside...Each corner is intended for one family, though sometimes it is occupied by more. On the inside, all around the building, is the bed platform, similar to the one in the potlatch house...A part of this however is used for storing their effects underneath it; many things are also kept. Especially their bark and fire wood, if they have any in advance. Below and in front of the platform is a low seat, six inches high, and three feet-wide, which is also similar to the one in the potlatch house...The fire is in front of this, and the smoke escapes by holes in the roof...Immediately over the fire, and about seven feet from the ground, sticks are placed in various positions, where food, especially fish and clams are hung to dry. This class of house, has now gone largely out of use, except by a few of the least civilized old ones.

Of the fourth type, the flat roof dwelling houses:

The sides are made both of upright and horizontal boards; and the roof is composed of two parts ...made of cedar shakes, or clap-boards, and which generally has quite a steep pitch, though not always as steep...and, second another part made of long boards...with barely enough pitch to carry off the rain. Such houses are not large, usually not far from twenty by twenty five feet, and are intended for only one or two families. The inside arrangement is very similar to those of the large dwelling houses. Twenty years ago there were several of these among the Twanas. Ten years ago they had all disappeared.

Of the fifth type, "civilized" houses:

The first on the Skokomish reservation were built about 1874 by the government carpenter with lumber bought by annuity money. They had floors and two or three rooms similar to small cottages for whites. Hence no further description is needed. They were generally about sixteen by twenty two feet. Since then the greater part of the Indians on the Sound have built for themselves civilized houses of some kind, often very much better than those first built by the government. Very few people now live on the ground in the smoke.

The sixth type, the summer houses or mat houses, were "made of mats, with occasionally a few boards. Generally they are built at fishing places during the summer. Inside the beds are laid around the side on boards a few inches from the ground. The fire is in the middle; most of the

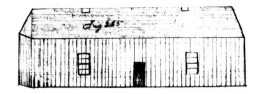

Above, house without floor belonging to Tenas John, a Klallam Indian, was 50 by 33 by 12 feet with upright boards for walls and coarse boards for roof in which were holes for escape of smoke.
Center, house of sawn lumber, belonging to Klallam chief, Balch, was 50 by 25 by 12 feet, without a floor.
Below, house of a Klallam, Carpenter John, was 24 by 15 by 10 feet with kitchen, porch, and chimney. This house had a floor. In those which had floors and no chimneys, holes were cut in floors for fireplaces and banks of earth built up between ground and floor. Sometimes floors were lined at fireplaces with tin. A few had truncated pyramids of boards 5 feet above fires. These extended through roofs to carry off smoke.

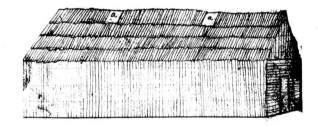

A common large house, varying up to 50 feet in length and 30 feet in width, owned by one man, but used by several families, usually one to a corner, separated by partial panels. Floorless houses of this type had doors either at ends or on one side of the structures. Around inside walls were bed platforms under which personal articles and firewood were stored. Each family had a fire, smoke from which escaped through holes in the roof at *aa*. This type of house was largely obsolete by 1894 except among a few older people.

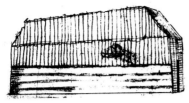

Front view (above) and side view of flat-roof dwelling intended for two families. Inside arrangement of these houses (which disappeared by the mid-1880's) was similar to that of the large dwelling house. One portion of the two-part roof shown above is that with a steep pitch of cedar shakes or clapboards; that seen in the side view below is another roof portion of long boards with just enough pitch to carry off rain. Sides were constructed of upright and horizontal boards.

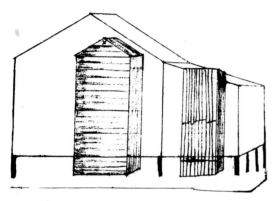

Outside view of two chimneys made wholly of boards. At base that on left was 7 by 7½ feet, and that on the right, 3 by 4 feet. Reason for large base size was to prevent side boards from burning. Sometimes sheet iron or broken stove parts were placed against inside chimney walls. Base was large enough to lay sick person inside chimney near the fire. Hearth was earth raised to floor level. Few chimneys were of brick, stone, or mud as natives had trouble making fireplaces with good draughts. Stoves became common about 1890. Eells saw transition from holes in roofs, to truncated pyramid flues above fires, to chimneys and finally, stoves.

Wooden doorlatch with a string to raise latch from outside. Some Indians used American locks.

space overhead is occupied with fish which are being dried. People and things are stowed where any room can be found, and the whole atmosphere is filled with smoke."

Of the seventh type, which Eells termed "the half-circle camp," he wrote: "When traveling in stormy weather they often place poles in the ground in the form of a semicircle to the windward and fasten mats to them, the whole standing so as to answer both as wall and roof. Under this shelter they sleep. The fire is to the leeward, which is open."

Finally, of the eighth type, tents of cotton cloth, he wrote that they "are now often used in travelling, and sails are also spread over poles so as to form a kind of low tent."

Outbuildings consisted of "barns, stables for horses, stables for oxen when they are logging, cellars and caches for roots (chiefly potatoes), woodsheds, and hen houses, the last two rather scarce. They often take their canoes into their large houses. These outhouses are all built after the style of those of the whites, though not usually as substantial. None of them were in use, as far as I know, before the coming of the whites..."

Tracing some of the changes which had taken place in materials used in making permanent buildings, he wrote:

Of late sawed boards are usually obtained. Barns and other out houses are generally made of split cedar boards from three to ten feet long. Formerly planks were made of cedar boards and as cedar decays very slowly, some of these are still in use among the older and less civilized Indians. The largest which I have seen were among the Clallams at Elwha. One was two and a half feet wide, and forty feet-long, and another three and a half feet wide, and twenty long. Such boards were split with wedges and trimmed by hewing...

Two important appurtenances to dwelling which Eells described were doors and fireplaces. Of the former:

An ancient form of door was a circular aperture cut through the building. The only one I have seen in their houses was in a Clallam house at Sequim. It was three and a quarter by three quarters feet...It was closed by sliding other boards over the aperture. In the house sent to the Exposition...the door is of the same style, but is closed by a single board a little larger than the aperture, which hangs over it being held there by a thong. In their summer houses...the doors consisted of mats hung over the entrance. At present all doors to their permanent houses are made after the style of the whites and are hung with good iron hinges, or when these cannot be obtained, with some kind of a rough wooden one...[They] often nail up their doors when they have no lock.

Of fireplaces he noted that in early times "the Clallams at least dug a circular place about a foot deep and five or six feet in diameter in the ground, in some of the houses, heaping up the dirt around the edge, upon which they sat or lay. There are none of these in use now, nor have there been for twenty years." He noted that in several of their houses

they build their fires on the ground, without any preparation, except the making the smoke hole in the roof. This often was about three feet-square, and generally had a cover, which might be used, when a severe storm occurred or when the occupants were absent...Occasionally in the houses which have floors of lumber, holes are cut in for fire places three or four feet square, about the middle of the room, the space from the ground to the floor being filled with earth, and perhaps the edges of the floor around the fireplace are lined with tin, while a hole is made in the roof, where the smoke may escape...Another form has occasionally been adopted from the white logging camps. The fire place is like that last described, but the place for the escape of smoke is quite different. A truncated pyramid is made of boards, hollow, so that the base, which is about five feet-square hangs some five feet above the fire, while the smaller end passes through the roof. The draught through this is sufficient to cause the smoke to pass through it, and thus the room is kept tolerably free from it. These have been used but seldom, and I have seen none for several years. They have been a transition affair from smoke to chimneys and stoves, when the Indians were unable to procure the latter...

Other appurtenances which Eells mentioned were ladders, which he found uncommon, and totem posts, even moreso, the nearest approach to them, the tamanous posts which he described in a chapter on religion. Of cupboards he wrote: "These were probably not in use until the coming of the whites." Tables were "an innovation from the whites."

Suggested Reading

Smith, Marian W. *The Puyallup-Nisqually, Columbia University Contributions in Anthropology,* XXXII, New York, 1940.

Kroeber, A.L. "American Culture and the Northwest Coast," *American Anthropologist*, New Series, XXV, 1 (January, 1923).

Waterman, T.T. "Some Conundrums in Northwest Coast Art," *American Anthropologist,* XXV, 4 (October, 1923).

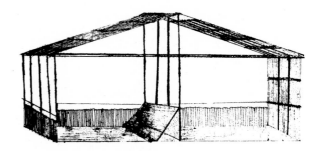

Stable for oxen for logging. *b*, was a manger in the stable, and the other half of building was for hay storage. Shelter was only on south (on right in illustration) side to protect from rain.

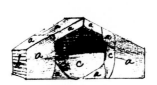 

Summer house, usually at a fishing place was constructed of *aa* mats; *b*, boards; and *c*, cloth. Inside, beds, slightly elevated, were laid around the wall; a fire was built in the center and fish were hung overhead, making a crowded, smoke-filled dwelling.
Summer house on right is wholly of mats.

Above, a "cellar." The 8 by 11-foot double-walled, dirt-insulated shed covered a shallow excavation. This type was little used because of river overflows. Below, potatoe cache, built of supports at each end holding ridgepole over which boards slanted and the whole finished as at center, was covered with several inches of dirt to protect potatoes from frost and rain. (Ruled lines were on the paper used by Eells for sketching.)

4: CLOTHING

In all of his chapters dealing with the material culture of the Indians, Eells described both that of an earlier period and that of his period of residency among them when such things were to a considerable extent of American manufacture. Since clothing was no exception, he found it unnecessary to describe at length that which was so commonplace by his time, devoting instead considerable space to the native clothing of an earlier era. Since little of that clothing remained in his day, the missionary depended considerably for its description on writings of white men who observed such cultural items before his time. In his notebooks he made no sketches of native clothing, only a few accessories, although Eells did include a few photographs of Indians in native garb of deer and mountain goat skins.

Although he prefaced his discussion of clothing with the observation that nearly all the Indians dressed in "civilized clothing," he did note by way of exception that

> a large share of the older women seldom wear hats or bonnets. They either go bareheaded or put a handkerchief or shawl over their heads. Once in a long while one is seen with a native hat. The old men, and a good share of the women go barefoot, as well as many children when they are not at school, and once in a long while a person is seen with moccasins. Occasionally a man is seen with a blanket on over his other clothes, but not often. Young children are often more scantily clothed than with the whites...

In contrast to materials of American manufacture, those of which the natives were originally clothed were of "deer, elk, bear and wild cat skins, dog's hair, hawk and eagle feathers, duck and geese down, the down of cotton from the fire-weed, cedar bark and roots, wool from the mountain goat, cattail rush, and sinew from the whale and deer."

Clothing items which Eells first described were those for the head, one kind of which—hats—were

> made by the Makahs, but many of them found their way up the Sound...It was water-tight, very serviceable, and seems to be made in a manner similar to the water-tight baskets...Other hats, somewhat similar, were made by the British Columbia Indians, especially the Nittinats and Nanaimos which were likewise imported. They were much flatter at the top. Those were worn as much by the women as the men, but commonly the Puget Sound Indians went bareheaded, as they made nothing of the kind.

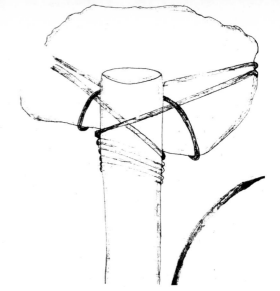

Clothing was made of leather worked with stones. Some stones were hafted as in this sketch; others not. On right is stick on which skin was placed to remove hair.

Puget Sound natives stored clothing in grass baskets which were pliable and more like bags than baskets. This is one imported from Quinaults.

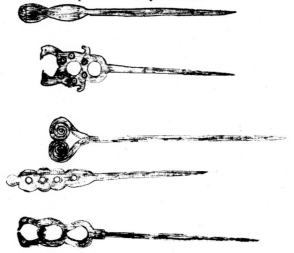

Fastenings, 5 to 6 inches long were used for blankets and shawls. Top one is wood and made by a Twana; next two down are brass, made by Klallams; next to bottom is iron used by a Twana; and bottom is bone, made by a Klallam.

As to head coverings for infants: "One kind, and the only native kind I have seen was made of cedar bark split into strips about half an inch wide, and woven at right angles, nearly into the shape of a bonnet. These were placed over the head and face of the infant, when fastened on to its board to keep out the smoke and dust..." Then, of headdresses:

> One kind was made of beaten cedar bark. A band of this, a half an inch to an inch in diameter, was made long enough to go around the head. Two bunches of the same material hung down behind, and two long feathers of eagles or hawks, stood erect on each side of the head...still another style I have seen was made of cloth, a cloth band being placed around the head, with strips of red cloth, a foot or more long, hanging down around so thickly that the face and neck were entirely concealed.

He also noted that a "kind of bonnet was made of the mountain goat" which was woven for the wives and daughters of chiefs. There was also "a woman's headdress...made from the wool of the mountain goat," and another headpiece from "the dentalia shell strung together from eight to a dozen wide, with beads or leather between the different rows."

He next described what he termed "body clothing," having read that when Vancouver visited the Klallams in 1792 he had reported those natives as clothed in skins of deer, bear, and other animals, but principally in well-made woolen garments of their own manufacture, probably, the missionary believed, women's woolen skirts. He also learned from Wilkes about leather hunting shirts fringed with beads or shells, and of a few leggings worn. Eells was never able to ascertain if the style of coats and pants made in former times of deer and elk skins had been patterned after those of white men. At any rate, by his time they had gone out of style.

He noted a coat made of cattail rushes which extended "down before and behind from the shoulders half way from the hips to the knees and...fastened together at the sides." "There was," continued Eells, "a hole from the neck and one for each arm and it was put on over the head. It shed rain well." He had never seen any like them until 1892 when he had two of them made for the World's Columbian Exposition.

Dresses for women were

> of at least two kinds [—] cedar bark, and the wool of the mountain goat. The latter was the dress of the wives and daughters of the chiefs, the former of the common people. It consisted of a skirt fastened in front around the waist. This was made by fastening to a band which went around the waist, twisted strings of the same material, which hung down for a foot and a half to two and a half feet...

Alderwood dish for grease, made by British Columbia Indians, was imported by Klallams. It was 9½ by 11 by 3½ inches deep, ornamented at top with shell inlay and thunderbird incised at each end.

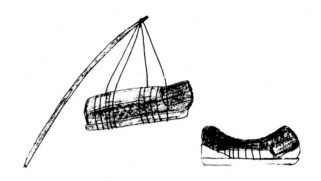

Another form of infant rocker. The child is covered with cloth and tied to a board and suspended from a pole.

Above is bone implement used for pressing woven parts in basket making. Handle is wrapped with cloth to prevent hand injury.

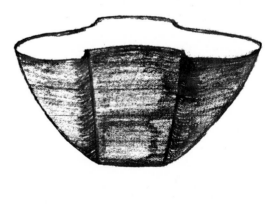

Wooden grease-holding dishes made by Klallams.

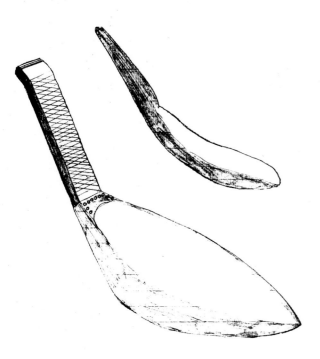

Spoons were made of maple or laurelwood, also from cattle horns. Large ladles were used to bring semi-liquid food to the mouth where it was pushed into it with smaller ladle or stick. A few were in use by 1890, but they had not disappeared as had wooden plates. Before use of cattle horns for spoons, mountain sheep horns were used.

This 3-foot-long ironwood needle was used for making mats of cattail rushes, cut by women in July and August and sun-dried. These rushes were tied in bunches convenient for carrying.

Mat needle made of ulna bone of an albatross. It was imported to Skokomish Reservation from Quinaults among whom it was a common implement.

A cape for Eells to take to the Exposition was made by a Twana woman from a blanket of mountain goat wool, which covering, Snohomish Indians had recently brought to the Skokomish Reservation. Eells later obtained a much shorter one—about a foot and a half long, as he described it, but very much heavier, the strands being much thicker and "very old" and evidently "the old fashion." Another "was of the same pattern, but of beaten cedar bark;" yet another was of the same material, "but only a foot or so wide" hanging "down in front like an apron," and worn "by the very poorest and the slaves."

Never one to moralize about the summertime scantiness of native clothing, the missionary, Eells, left that sort of thing to his sources. First, Wilkes whose observation appeared in the notes as follows: "Although the dress of these natives would seem to offer some concealment to the body, few are seen that wear it with any kind of decency. Their persons are usually very filthy and they may be said at all times to be coated with dirt." Then, Gibbs whose observations also appear in the notes:

They also wore on occasions, robes made of small animals, such as the rabbit, sewelell (Aplodontia leporina) muskrat &c, or of larger ones as the cougar and beaver. The women universally wore a breech clout of strands gathered round the waist, and falling usually to the knees which served the purpose of concealment. With the men no idea of immodesty prevailed. Decency had not even its fig leaf. The clout was sometimes made of twisted grass, at others of cedar bark, hackled, and split into a fringe. The ordinary dress however of the men, when they saw fit to use any, was a deer skin shirt, leggings and moccasins...

Blankets were of at least three types:

One was made of dog's hair, geese or duck down, and the cotton from the fireweed. These were twisted into strings and woven together. This special breed of dog was kept for its hair, but is now extinct. It was not large, but the hair was long, and a woman's wealth was often estimated by the number of such dogs she owned. I have never seen any of these blankets. Vancouver speaks of the blanket as resembling those of Pomerania but larger. They were white.

Another kind of blanket was imported from the Makahs who made it. It was made from the inner bark of the cedar slightly beaten, so as not to be too stiff, and woven with strings of geese down twisted. The only one I have seen was at Dungeness in 1878, and had a border or fringe of black hair.

The third kind was of the wool of the mountain goat twisted into coarse strings and woven together...

All of these blankets were woven on a loom...

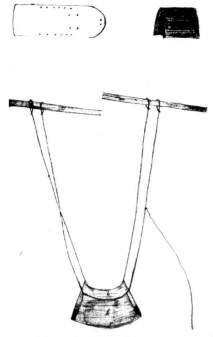

Above left, infant's board with hole through which strings were passed to tie on the child. Above right, cap of woven cedar bark usually imported by Klallams and Makahs to put over head and face to protect children from smoke and dirt.
Below, infant's rocker made with ropes attached to posts and to the ropes, a blanket in which the child's bed was placed in blanket and swung with string attached to one rope.

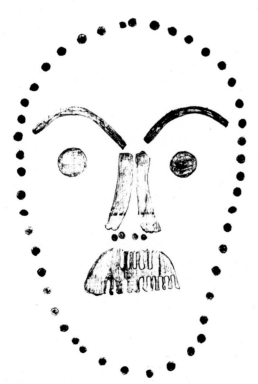

Board carved with rough looking face to frighten crying child into silence when worn by parents as a mask. This was made by a Klallam.

Eells wrote that robes were made "of the skins of the deer, elk, bear, whistling marmot and wild cat, the latter being sewed together. Occasionally a buffalo robe was obtained from the Klikitat Indians." Of hand and arm clothing he could not learn "of any special covering," assuming that some "parts of the blankets and body clothing" would naturally protect these parts. Of leg and foot clothing, moccasins were occasionally used, "but the climate is too wet to admit their being worn with much comfort, nor is the cold in the winter so great that they need them long. They generally went barefooted. At present the Twana women spend much time in knitting woolen socks, which they sell to the whites. Wilkes and Gibbs speak of leggings, occasionally." Of parts of dresses: "Fastenings for blankets and shawls are and were made of wood, bone, iron and brass, sometimes very plain and common, and sometimes with ornamental heads, as dogs, birds and the like. They were five or six inches long..." Fringes "were appended to the buckskin coats, pants and shirts. They were about an inch long, and made likewise of buckskin." Receptacles for dresses were the baskets he had previously described.

Suggested Reading

Howay, F. W. "The Dog's Hair Blankets of the Coast Salish," *Washington Historical Quarterly,* IX, 2 (April, 1918).
Curtis, Edward B. *The North American Indian,* IX, New York, 1913.

Mat blocks were made of alder or maplewood 5 to 7 inches long and about 3 inches wide at the middle. One end was handle and the other, the working end which was curved on under side.

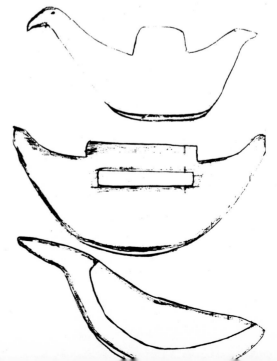

5: FURNITURE, VESSELS, AND UTENSILS OF HOUSEHOLD USE

In this chapter Eells described the various and numerous articles used in the operation of the Indian household. As in his other chapters, he made little attempt to interpret the topics he discussed. However, an inescapable by-product of the chapter is the revelation of the natives' familiarity with the natural environment which offered them materials to skilfully fabricate for their own use or for trade. As in other aspects of their material culture, Eells by his descriptions and sketches revealed the acculturation process at work as the Indians adopted these kinds of white men's goods.

The first objects described were beds. These

were made from common mats and blankets. The mat is partly rolled up which forms the pillow. The rest becomes the bed... When there are several thicknesses of these mats, the bed is quite soft and comfortable. Old fashioned blankets of dog's hair and other material, skins were used for covering. But a bed entirely of these materials is never seen now, although the mats are used to some extent now by the poorer and older Indians as the lower part of the bed. Those of feathers, straw, springs, with sheets, quilts, American blankets and feather pillows are very common. Their bedsteads—the bed platforms...are being largely supplanted by bedsteads of American style, both homemade and boughten.

A counterpart to native mats were rugs made after whites came and fabricated by Indian women almost exclusively from rugs. These were of three types:

(1) The rags, cut in strips, are braided and then sewed into rugs of a circular or oblong form. (2) They are torn in strips, and these are woven with a warp and woof. They are both rectangular and circular or oblong and are made with a little taste in the arrangement of colors, more than with the first style, but far less than with the third. They are by far the most serviceable of the three kinds. Both the rectangular and circular are made on the floor...The rectangular ones may also be made while hanging on the wall...I have two or three times also seen them in a kind of loom similar to the one anciently used in making blankets. (3) The most ornate kind is made by taking a piece of burlap, as the ground work, stretching it on a frame and drawing rags through it by means of an instrument similar to a large crochet needle of iron. By so doing they can draw rags of any color into any place, and thus they often make rude forms of men, animals, trees, and various

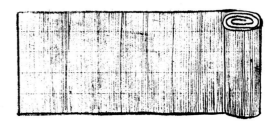

From sloughs and inlets native women gathered reeds to make mats for various uses. One was bed seen here with one end rolled for a pillow. In Eells' time but few people—the poor and the old—used mats as underparts of beds.

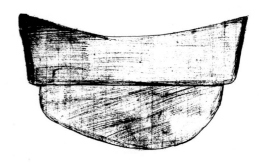

Fish knife, native-made, with wood handle and sheet iron blade.

Stone dish used by Klallams for holding oil.

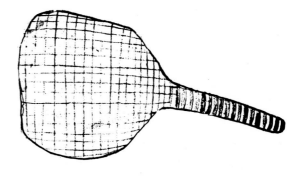

Baby rattle made of small slits of wood by Squaxin Indian to form a closed basket. Stones were put inside for noise making.

figures...I can learn of no different names in the Twana language, by which the three kinds are called. They use these in their own houses and sell them to the whites.

These rugs, however, did not entirely replace native mats which were considerably more varied in form than were rugs, for Eells noted several kinds. Some were

made of grass of the cattail rush. This grass is cut by the women in July and August, dried in the sun, and tied in bunches as large as can be comfortably carried. When a woman finds time to make mats, she assorts her rushes into three lots according to size. Of the longest rushes she makes the largest mats, which are about five feet wide and twelve to twenty long. Of rushes of medium length, she makes mats about three feet wide and from eight to fifteen feet long. Of the smaller stalks she makes mats about two feet wide and from two to four long. The largest mats are used chiefly for lining wooden houses in constructing mat houses. Those of medium size are used at times for the same purpose, for the half-circle camps, for beds, pillows, seats, table covers, and as substitutes for umbrellas and oil-cloth, two layers forming an almost complete protection from the rain. The narrowest mats, usually from 3 to 4 feet long, are used mostly for cushions, as in canoes and for paddlers to kneel on. While sorting over the rushes, she splits off a small part from the base of the stalk of which she makes a string which she uses in sewing the mat together.

The two wider kinds are also quite an article of commerce with the Makah and British Columbia Indians, who make none of this kind, but who value them as superior to those of their own manufacture which are of cedar bark. The raw material is also used as an article of trade.

Of the manufacture of these types of mats, formerly a large part of the indoor work of women:

The rushes, having been sorted, are cut, so as to be of a uniform length, as long as the mat is to be wide. The ends of the rushes are first temporarily fastened together in the shape of the mat, then strings made of the same material, shredded and twisted, are passed transversely through these rushes, and about 2½ inches apart. This is done with a needle of hard wood 3 feet long, half an inch wide, three-cornered, and with an eye in one end, in which the string is placed. After the string is passed through, a small piece of wood with a crease in it, is pressed over the mat where the strings are, to render it firm and of good shape. The edges of the mat are fastened by weaving the ends of the transverse threads firmly together.

Another mat type was "made and used in a manner similar to the medium-sized cattail mat, but it is made from a round rush which usually

Awls were used as leather punches in making clothing.

Long before Eells lived among them, natives wore clothing made from cedar bark. Implement shown here was wooden hackler for beating bark fine into workable material. In Eells' time it was used for hackling cedar bark and for other purposes. Some hacklers were made of whalebone.

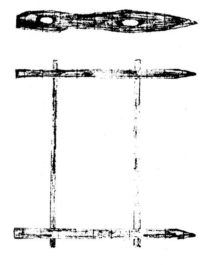

A loom Eells saw in use by a Klallam woman making a rug. Two posts about four feet long, six inches wide and half that thickness were sharpened on one end and driven into the ground. Cross bars were inserted in pairs of holes, one above and the other lower down.

grows to a height only sufficient to make mats 3 feet wide. This rush is about a third of an inch in diameter. It is not very common." There is also a "rough mat...made from the inner bark of cedar, split into strips half an inch wide or thereabouts and woven together at right angles. It is used chiefly to lay fish upon when they are cleaned or to place on a frame over a fire on which food is placed to dry." Another "good" mat was made by Makah and British Columbia women from the inner bark of the cedar:

This is split into strips a quarter or a third of an inch wide, and woven in a manner similar to the last, but much larger, more firmly, and with carefully finished edges. Sometimes the strips are colored black, which are woven in at regular distances, or else the border is made of black strips. These mats are rectangular and usually about four feet by seven or eight, though some are larger and some are smaller. They are used for lining houses, and on floors, and they are placed on the ground for tables and seats. For bedding they are considerably inferior to the rush mats, as there is far less elasticity to them; neither are they as good as a protection against rain, but they are superior for sails, as they are far lighter.

The last mat, a small table type, also made by Makah and Quinault women, found its way among the Sound Indians and was highly prized by whites. These were

both round and oblong is shape, seldom more than fifteen inches long or less than six inches in diameter. They are made from a very fine grass woven very firmly and colored very prettily, at present with aniline dyes. They make a useful, ornamental, and substantial article for the table. I have seen a few similar to these made by the Puyallup and Twana Indians, but they were far inferior to those made by the two tribes on the coast.

Eells was of the opinion that the four mat types he first described were made almost exclusively by the Sound Indians and those further to the south. He thought it not strange that they should be made by these Indians, for, unlike the Makahs, they had the necessary materials growing in their lands. He did think it strange that Sound Indians did not make cedar bark mats, because cedar was available to them and they used its bark for many other purposes. He thought it generally known "that the dividing line between the Makahs and Clallams about the Hoko river, is also the dividing line between the manufacture of these different kinds of mats. When made however they do not remain on their respective sides of the line, but are often traded with each other, as their respective merits are fully recognized by the different tribes."

Other native household items as seats, tables, tubs, washing vessels, and brooms (Eells wondered if brooms formerly had been used very much.) had, as he explained it, yielded by his time to those of American manufacture. Some of them were giving way to comparable American items at differing rates. Native ladles, for instance, were going out of use as rapidly as native plates, the latter of three kinds—wood [usually alder], horn, and stone and used mainly for holding fish and oil. Ladles were

made both of wood, maple or laurel being preferred, and the horns of cattle. Before the introduction of cattle a few of horns came with horn dishes from the north [British Columbia] and the east [near and beyond the Cascade Mountains]. The bowl of these ladles is generally five or six inches long, three or four wide, and an inch deep, though those for children are much smaller. These ladles were used for semi-liquid food; but are not always placed in the mouth, but near the mouth, and the food is pushed from them into the mouth with a small stick, or taken from them with a smaller ladle, which is placed in the mouth.

He was unaware that they had ever used table knives or forks unless at times they had used their hunting knives, for, as he commented, "Fingers were made before forks, and used too. Now American ones are very common." From attending Indian feasts, he observed both native and American materials used for napkins. The native material was

of cedar bark, slightly beaten, about 2 feet long and tied into bunches an inch in diameter. I have seen also a piece of calico thirty or forty feet-long stretched by two individuals from end to end along a row of feasters, behind their backs. When they had finished their meal, with a sudden jerk it was flopped over their heads in front of them, when all at the same time wiped their hands and mouths, when it was flopped back as suddenly, and the work was done...

He was aware that the growing scarcity of ingeneous and well made goods of native manufacture was beginning to be reflected in their enhanced money value on both the native and American markets. A case in point were their prized "kerf" (a word Eells did not use) boxes whose manufacture he thought "peculiar." In one of these boxes for holding water

The four sides are made of one board; where the corner is to be a small miter is cut, both on the inside and outside, partly through. Then the corners are steamed and bent at right angles, and the inside miter is cut so perfectly that it fits watertight when the corners are bent. The corner where the two ends of the board meet are then fastened with wooden pegs driven in diagonally. The top and bottom of the box are fastened on with pegs similarly inserted.

Among natives utensils which increased in value were baskets, although their value depended on the quality of materials used in their manufacture and the skill with which they were made. Eells categorized these into twelve types some of which were made by Indians of his acquaintance and some imported from other peoples:

(1) The water-tight basket [generally] ...oval at the rim...made from cedar roots, and grass, woven and sewed together, are very stiff, and are the most useful and substantial baskets they have. All the Sound tribes give them the same name Spa-tco or spû-tco, except the Nisqually speaking tribes. They are made by a very few women and are still valued highly from three to five dollars apiece for those holding half a bushel or more. They usually hold from two quarts to a bushel, though a few very small ones are made, holding only about a pint. They are very useful for carrying water and juicy berries. Formerly they were used for cooking; stones having been heated and placed in the water in them, with the food. They are also used for carrying and storing dry articles as potatoes, apples, dry fish and the like. They are usually ornamented with some artistic figure.

(2) A stiff basket, but not water-tight, about the same size as the last, is made of grass and cedar bark. This kind is woven, not sewed, and is used for carrying and storing dry articles, and for work less wearing and rough than the water-tight basket. They are not much ornamented.

(3) The cedar limb basket. Cedar limbs are split and the bark having been taken off usually, are woven together and thus a common basket for carrying and storing common dry articles is made. They generally hold from a half a bushel to a bushel and a half.

(4) The fancy basket. This is made entirely of small grass, woven, and tightly pressed together, often with a small bone implement, or some similar instrument. A part of the grass is colored, and with this the basket is ornamented. It usually holds from two quarts to a bushel and is used as a ladies work basket, or for storing cloth and fancy articles. Very few have handles...

(5) Another basket is made of a bush as the hazel, split and shaved on both sides. The pieces are from a third to half an inch wide and are woven together at right angles. This kind is used rather more by the whites than the Indians, as a clothes basket and was I think originally a copy from some American basket.

(6) Another kind is made from the grass of the cattail rush woven together. It usually holds about a bushel. It is not durable as the rush is easily broken. It is not often made or used, except as a temporary affair, and occasionally for storing their effects.

(7) A large carrying basket...made by the Makah and Quinaielt Indians, and imported by those on the Sound, those living nearest these two tribes, naturally using more than the more distant neighbors. These are made of small round sticks about an eighth of an inch in diameter, split in two, and placed about a quarter of an inch apart. Others are placed somewhat similarly to these, but at right angles with them, and then they are fastened together with bark. They are thus more open than any other basket made, but very serviceable. They usually hold near a bushel, and are used for carrying and storing nearly all kinds of dry articles.

(8) The Makahs also make a fancy basket, which does not usually hold over two quarts. It also finds its way up the Sound and is also prized quite highly by the whites for it is the best made fancy basket in use on the Sound...It is however made in a variety of shapes and often with covers. It is made of fine grass, the same that is used in making their table mats. It is highly ornamented, some the grass being colored with aniline dyes. Formerly they used their native colors for this purpose, but they have been entirely abandoned, as inferior. They are used by the women for holding sewing material and similar articles.

(9) A basket is made by the Makah and British Columbia Indians, of cedar bark, split into strips a third or half an inch wide and woven together in much the same way as the cedar bark mats. They often hold a bushel or more, though some are much smaller, and are used for storing light articles. They are not strong and will not bear much rough usage. On this account, very few find their way far up the Sound, the Clallams being the principal importers.

(10) A basket is made by the Quinaielt Indians of a fine grass which looks as much like a bag as a basket...It holds from half a bushel to a bushel and is used for storing cloth and similar articles. Only a few find their way to the Sound, they being more abundant among the Chehalis Indians than those further north.

(11) Another which looks like the last, but which is made of another kind of grass, comes from the Klikitat Indians east of the Cascade Mountains ...It seems to be made in a similar manner, and to be used for similar purposes to the last. Both are quite substantial.

(12) I have seen one or two baskets made by the Sound Indians of alder bark. The bark is simply taken from the young growth, five or six inches wide and doubled together, the sides being fastened with a string. They are a frail affair, and only made as a temporary basket when in the woods for want of something better.

Suggested Reading

Underhill, Ruth, *Indians of the Pacific Northwest*, Washington, 1944.

Smith, Marian W. *The Puyallup-Nisqually, Columbia University Contributions in Anthropology*, XXXII, New York, 1940.

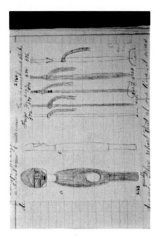

On the right are five 4-foot long hand sticks used for tamanousing for lost spirits. On the left is a 4-foot idol Eells saw in 1878. It had silver quarters nailed to it for eyes. It was without legs and feet and was set in the ground where performers made incantations around it.

These are head bands of beaten cedar bark ornamented with feathers. Eagle feathers were preferred, but those of hawks were substituted. In black tamanous ceremonials, bands were colored black, and feathers tipped with the same color. In other ceremonial forms, they retained their natural colors.

Cedar was in abundance on Puget Sound. Many items were made from it, one being a band of bark wound around the upper end of tamanous sticks as in the illustration above at the top right. These sticks were used to recover lost spirits stolen and taken to spirit world. To find a lost spirit prevented the loser from becoming ill. When not in use head bands such as in the illustration immediately above were hung on idols as in the picture above top right. These idols were kept hidden in the woods and brought out for ceremonial purposes.

Three "rude images of a man" placed in Twana grave houses. Each surmounted with cap or hat were without clothes, nose, mouth, eyes, ears or arms. Two were for grave of a chief.

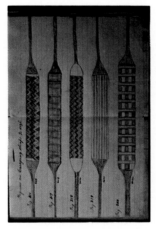

Straps used by all Sound tribes for carrying baskets and other loads. They were ornamented by weaving different colored strings in the straps.

Painted mask represented bird's head with feathers on top.

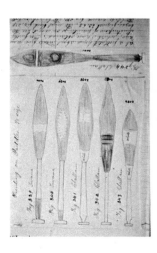

On the right, one man's tamanous painted on blade of canoe paddle. Usually paddle blade paintings like these above, Eells believed meaningless.

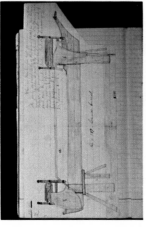

Canoe burial of prominent women taking place, October, 1877. Head and foot boards of her American bed were nailed one to each end of her burial canoe.

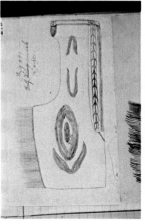

Wolf mask with hair on top.

Unfinished woven rugs. Rug making from rags was introduced by whites. Some circular ones, others rectangular, with some taste in color arrangements, were made on floors or from a hanging position. Few were made on looms which in earlier days had been used for making blankets.

Natives readily copied some processes from whites. One was rug making. Here an unfinished fancy rug was made by drawing rags through a stretched piece of burlap by means of a large iron needle. Natives used rugs in their own houses and also sold them to whites.

Wood carvings over windows and door of Tyee Charley's house on Skokomish Reservation. These carvings were painted red.

Puget Sound Indians made much use of abundant wood of their land. This is a watertight bucket. Sides were one board kerfed at corners, steamed and bent and fastened with wooden pegs at meeting-ends and to bottom and top boards cemented with native glue.

Eells copies these tattoo patterns from Twana women's wrists and hands excepting that of semicircles on a man's hands. They were made by drawing needles and blackened thread under the skin as deeply as the subject could bear, permanently marking the skin.

This is a soft, pliable basket used for storage. It was imported from Yakimas east of the Cascade Mountains.

Woven grass water-tight hat imported from Makahs. Puget Sound Indians usually went bareheaded as they made nothing of the kind according to Eells.

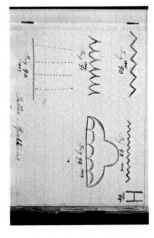

Beaded head band (aa, light pink beads; bb, white beads) such as this was occasionally sprinkled with white duck down for greater ornamentation.

Woven Twana cloth rug. Outside rim was not woven, but was of cloth binding.

6: PERSONAL ADORNMENT

In this chapter Eells described and sketched the objects natives used to adorn themselves. Although in no sense did he wish to provide a complete exposition of the practice, it is evident from his notes that the practice was contingent on not only such variables as time, space, and technology, but those of age, sex and class. As in other chapters, Eells endeavored, but only minimally, to illustrate and enliven his notes with accounts of Indian legendry.

He began his discussion by describing various types of skin ornamentation, first of which he entitled "Painting," of which he wrote:

> During their religious ceremonies, and often at their feasts, potlatches and at their gambling performances, they painted their faces. Red was the universal color, except at their black tamahnous ceremonies, when black was used. The women sometimes paint to prevent their being tanned, and if they have done anything which will make them blush in company, they sometimes paint to prevent these blushes being seen. They generally use their fingers for brushes, and have no especial pattern. Commonly they paint their cheeks and forehead smoothly, but sometimes in streaks, these running both ways of the face, also in spots in a very irregular manner. Formerly in time of war, they also painted profusely.

Another type of skin ornamentation appeared in the notes under the title "Tattooing." Of this practice, Eells observed: "This was common, but the younger ones do but little of it, as the whites, whose example they follow, do not tattoo." He doubted that natives followed the practice in pre-contact times, but thought they probably began it when whites, as sailors, and employees of the Hudson's Bay Company, were amongst them. He recorded that it was much more common on hands and wrists than on other parts of the body. He could not learn that there was any special meaning to the figures he sketched other than mere ornamentation. "In doing the work," he explained, "they use a needle and thread, blackening the thread, and drawing it under the skin, as deeply as they can bear it."

One legend the missionary included pertained to the source of paint for body decoration:

Native-made brass bracelet. Puget Sound Indians made brass and copper bracelets and purchased ones of silver made by Makahs and British Columbia Indians and by white Americans.

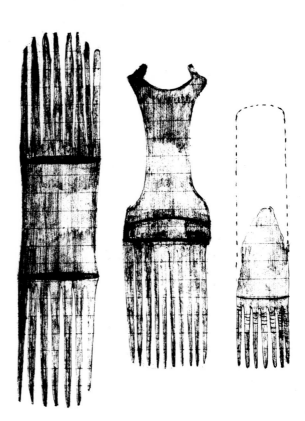

Native combs. One on right was made of horn. Single combs were more common than double ones.

Long ago before Dokibatl, the Great Changer, and Deity of these Indians first came to the Sound, this [east?] bank was Klikitat Indians, and the bank opposite on the other side of the Canal was Twanas. There was a great contest of gambling between the two tribes, and the Klikitats won the game. When Dokibatl came he changed them all to land. Because the Klikitats won, the Twanas now use this paint as a kind of charm in their dancing, gambling and religious ceremonies, that they may be successful. Because the Twanas were beaten, they are still beaten in their contest with other tribes, i.e. once beaten, always beaten.

Another source of red paint of superior quality was obtained from some clay further down the Sound by Klallams, although he thought it not "properly in their country." Another paint was obtained from the gnarl of a certain tree found in the mountains, but he could not ascertain what kind of tree it was. Other paints, he noted, were obtained from the juice of blackberries and raspberries, and one paint of white or yellowish color was obtained by burning, grinding an elk-horn and mixing it with oil.

Of head ornaments, ear pendants, worn by both men and women, were of three kinds: "…two of them being made from their money, the same as whites. One is of the dentalia shells, a number of which are fastened together…Small pieces of black on red cloth are often fastened in the lower part for greater ornament. The other is of abalone shell…" Eells saw but one stone ear pendant and that found in a grave at Hoodsport. Added Eells: "With the exception of a very few old Indians, they have been supplanted by American ones. One Clallam has become quite expert in making them of silver." As to copper ornaments, Eells wrote that Vancouver had reported many on natives up the Sound, but had not stated on what parts of the body they were worn. Eells narrated a tradition, somewhat reminiscent of the American Plains Indian Ghost Dance and of the Cargo Cult of the South Pacific, in which an old man journeyed north from Puget Sound with canoe, paddles, and cargo of copper to tell natives of those regions that they should die, but afterwards, rise and live again. Eells believed that copper obtained by Puget Sound Indians about him had come from British Columbia or Alaska where he wrote that it was said to have been mined.

Headbands were of dentalia, formerly used, although Eells implied that there still prevailed at potlatches the practice of sprinkling the head with the white down of ducks as an ornament. As to neck ornamentation:

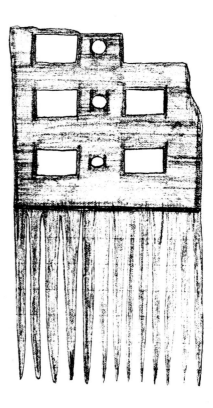

Puget Sound Indians were attentive to their hair. Combs were made of wood and bone, with teeth averaging 2½ inches in length with five teeth to the inch. Sixteen teeth were the most found by Eells' time on any one comb.

Necklaces were formerly made by stringing the dentalia and olivella shells. Sometimes these strings were five feet long, and were doubled several times. Dog fish bones and bear's claws were also strung for necklaces, the latter being used as charms. Beads of various styles, shapes, colors and sizes have taken the place of these old ornaments, some being very large. At first blue ones introduced by the Hudson's Bay Company, were almost exclusively used, but now these are going out of date and are almost as seldom used as the old native ones. Most of the girls now use but few more, or any different ones from white girls. They now usually keep their long strings of blue beads in their trunks or hanging in their houses with their keys fastened to them. The women and girls used these necklaces almost exclusively.

Breast ornaments were gorgets of dentalium which were formerly used. "I have seen," he wrote, "a few among the Indians on the Sound, but when in 1892 I wished to procure some for the Worlds Columbia Exposition, I had to send to Quinaielt for them…"

Of nose ornaments: "Formerly they bored a hole through the septum of the nose, in which they inserted polished bone or wood, quills or the dentalium shell, but they abandoned the practice so long ago that in twenty years I have only seen two or three very old ones with this hole, and none with the ornament."

Of ornaments of the limbs, he was

not aware that before the whites came they ever had any rings, bracelets or anklets, but they may have had them of copper, as copper was brought from British Columbia. Certainly as soon as the first whites came, they gladly obtained and used them, and made them from the best material they could procure, valuing them highly and burying both finger rings and bracelets with their dead. They make many from brass and copper and buy silver ones which are excellently made by the Makah and British Columbia Indians as well as those of American make…"

Eells noted that combs were made both of wood and bone, their teeth usually about two and a half inches long with about five to the inch, although they varied up to sixteen teeth, the most he had seen in a single comb. Single ones were more common than double ones and their heads were sometimes carved "somewhat artistically." He was told that soaps had formerly been made from a sugar-colored clay and of leaves of certain trees. He was also told that formerly perfumes had been made from sweet scented roots, but like so many other perfumes, they had been abandoned "long ago, for those of civilized manufacture."

Suggested Reading

Elmendorf, W. W. *The Structure of Twana Culture, Research Studies, Washington State University,* XXVIII, 3, Pullman, Washington, 1960.

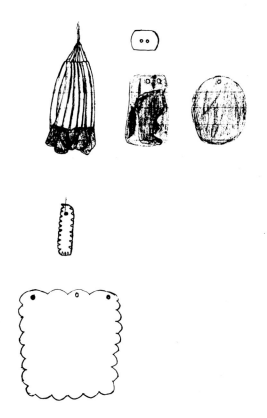

Various types of ear pendants. Above left is of dentalium shells with small pieces of red and black cloth fastened in lower portion for greater ornamentation. All others, excepting small serrated stone pendant, are of abalone shell. With the exception of older natives, most people by Eells' time used American ornaments.

7: IMPLEMENTS

In this chapter Eells described and sketched a great number of implements natives used for a variety of purposes in both peace and war. Special implements for catching fish and other food animals are described in this manuscript under the topic "Subsistence." Because of their durable nature Eells was able to record many of them from personal observation, for he had seen many of them in his travels and apparently had a sizeable collection of them.

The type of implements Eells first described were those which he entitled "Implements of General Use," foremost of which were knives of different kinds. One in common use among older Indians of his day had a bone handle with a curved steel blade, usually from an old rasp. Also made from an old rasp was a hunting knife, double-edged with two pieces or iron riveted on. Another knife was made entirely of bone. He had in his possession one seven and a half inches long tapering to a point, and intended mainly for cutting open skins in dressing slain animals. Another type was of slate stone, two of which Eells had in his possession. Other types of knives which he had seen or had in his possession were hybrid-like of wood or stone attached to metal blades, although he had apparently seen a double-edged all-bone knife some seventeen inches long and an inch and a half wide and a quarter-inch thick. This instrument had been used for debarking cedar trees. Of knives, axes, adzes and celts in general:

> The old style was made of stone of which I have obtained about twenty-five. I believe that these represent about all shapes and sizes which were in general use. They vary in length from three to seven inches, in width from three fourths to three and a quarter inches, in thickness from three eighths to three fourths of an inch, and in weight from one and a half to twelve ounces. All are polished, with one exception...Most of them are of metamorphic rock, and a few of sedimentary, and two of hard sandstone. Generally they are sharpened by being ground more on one side than on the other, but a few are sharpened entirely on one side. I have obtained them both from Clallam, Twana and Squakson Indians, from Clallam Bay to the head of Hood Canal, and across the Isthmus to Squakson island. Generally they are flat on one side and rounded on the other; but two are rounded on both sides. Some Indians say that these were used as hatchets or axes, for ordinary chopping, and there are trees near Dewatte and Dosewailopsh which have been partially or wholly cut down by such axes. Others say that they were used as hand adzes, with which to hollow their canoes, after they had been hollowed by burning. Such

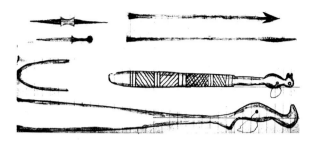

At one time war clubs were part of Sound natives' arsenals. These are sketches Eells made of miniature war clubs made for him by Klallams.

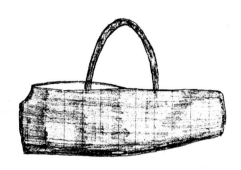

Natives used parts of many animals and birds to fashion useful items. This is quiver made of bearskin. Wolfskins were used for same purpose.

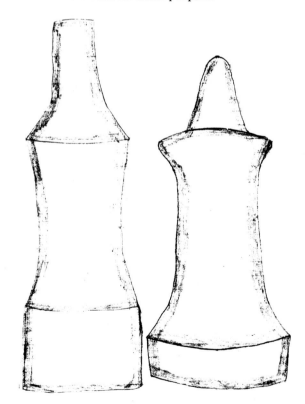

According to Eells, natives used stone to fashion stone hammers of sedementary, quartzite and basaltic stone.

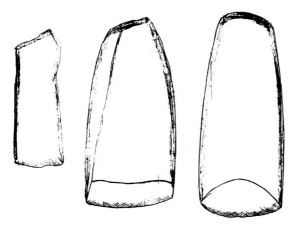

From abundant stone of the Pacific Northwest, natives made many tools and implements. Here are two stone axes and one hatchet. Although Eells obtained these from Indians, he said all axes, adzes and celts, then in use, were of "civilized manufacture" with exception of one style of hand adze.

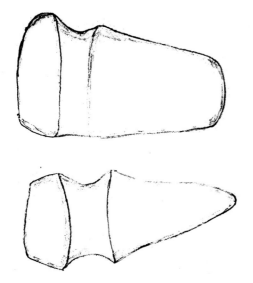

Axe found at Tacoma. Finished like those in the Mississippi Valley, according to Eells, it was made of stone.

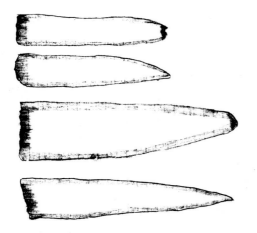

Wedges made of elk horn. Other materials used in making wedges were wood and stone.

adzes are now in common use, only they are made of old rasps and hafted with wooden handles...I have one hafted as an adze for the Columbia Exposition, but have not seen an Indian who professed to know how to haft them as an axe...I have seen one [handle] with a bird's head at one end...

Of whetstones, Eells wrote that he had

often seen them [use]...a small black roundish, irregular stone, similar to many beach stones in shape though I have not seen such on the beach. It has a very firm smooth grain. Some Indians have told me they find them on the beach, while others say that they bring them from the northern shores of the Straits of Fuca. It is plain that they had no use for exactly such before the introduction of metallic tools by the whites, though they did probably use something similar to sharpen their stone axes.

Wedges were of three types: wood, stone, and elk horn. Those he had seen of the latter, varied in length from five to fourteen inches, and in diameter, from one to two and a half inches, generally sharpened more on one side than on the other, and sometimes entirely on one side. He observed that occasionally elderly Indians used native hammers of stone, but among most of the people iron and steel had generally superseded them. Older hammers generally weighed from three to three and a half pounds, and were from six to seven inches long. There were some exceptions to these dimensions. The only awls he had seen were of wood or bone.

Eells introduced a section entitled "War and the Chase" with an account of warfare in which implements were used:

War when possible was carried only by treachery and stealth. About twenty-five years ago the Clallams of Dungeness had what they called a great battle with the Tsimpsheans [Tsimshians] of British Columbia, Sept. 21, 1867 [1868]. Eighteen of the latter were camped on Dungeness spit, when a Clallam was sent apparently as a friend to visit them. In reality he was a spy. When he returned he reported their strength. In the night when the Tsimpsheans were asleep, the Clallams went to their camp and massacred all but one of them who escaped, she having been left for dead, but recovered. This was a great battle...The whole twenty six [of the attacking Klallams] were afterwards taken through the help of Hon. J. G. Swan, and carried to the Skokomish reservation, where they were placed in irons and kept at hard labor by Charles King the Indian agent. The Tsimshean woman was kept by the wife of Benjamin Ranie of Dungeness, who was also a Tsimshean, until she fully recovered, when she was sent to her home, with a large number of presents from the United States Government, which satisfied them, so that they never retaliated.

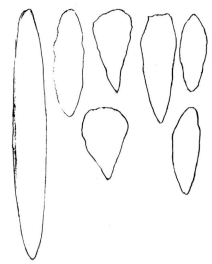

Twana spearheads. That on left was lancehead from Chehalis Indians. Second from upper left was made of obsidian and Eells believed it to have been imported.

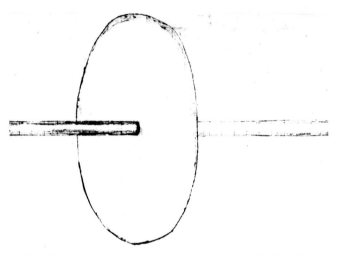

Implement used for spinning yarn, formerly for blankets and woolen clothing. Circular whorl is board, 6 or 7 inches in diameter through center of which ran a two-foot-long stick. Whorl was spun by holding it in one hand and rolling it on thigh, while yarn was held in other hand. By Eells' time whorls were made of tin lard pail covers. Indians would not use American spinning wheels introduced to them when agents came among them.

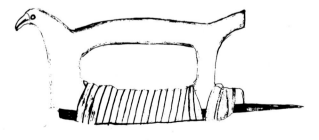

Hand adze used by Klallams at Elwha. Handle was of bone, with cloth binding.

Among various "weapons for striking," were war clubs of four materials: copper, stone, bone and wood. Eells claimed to have had a copper one in his possession. Another such club, twenty-two inches long, two inches wide and seven-sixteenths of an inch at the handle and weighing three pounds, was traced to British Columbia where it was formerly worth three slaves. Battle axes, mainly of stone, were used for cutting and striking. When he showed a sixteen-inch one to an old Indian "it made his eyes sparkle, and seemed to fill him with new life as he went through the war like motions, and showed in how still a manner they formerly crept up to kill a sleeping enemy." The missionary also noted that the carving on all of them was intended to represent the head of the thunderbird, an emblem of power, designed to inspire the warrior with courage. He depended on a Twana schoolboy, working under direction of his father, for sketches of old war clubs. The same lad also drew for him two war spears, the head of one made of lead, which meant to Eells that it had been made in the post-contact period. The head of the other, which the lad sketched, was of bone. Eells thought one of obsidian, found near the head of Hood Canal, to have been imported, possibly from eastern Oregon.

Another weapon of war, firepots, were

said to have been formerly used to set on fire houses into which an enemy had fled. Some vessel, perhaps a basket, was filled with pitchwood. A part of the besieging party would attack one side of the house, in order to draw the attention of the besieged to the opposite side, when the force, which had these fire pots would approach, set fire to them, throw it on the roof, and as the besieged attempted to escape, they were killed with clubs, spears, bows and arrows.

Bows and arrows had by the missionary's time gone out of use except as playthings for children. Yet, but a short time before his coming they had been used in war. He told of the acquisition by a white man from a Nisqualli Indian of nearly a hundred arrows made to kill white people in the war of 1855-56:

These were pointed with iron, but the heads were fastened firmly in the shaft. The shaft was made of cedar wood, except...the lower end which was of bone in order to make that end heavier and so more sure of hitting the mark. The iron arrow point or head was fastened to this piece of bone...He [the white man] also has a bow, obtained at the same place, and made for the same war, the back of which is covered with sinew cemented on, which renders it very strong and elastic.

Eells thought the Sound region very poor in materials for making stone "arrow points" in contrast to that region along the Columbia. Again recounting native tradition: "The Twana Indians have a tradition that these of stone were made by the wolf or panther, while those beasts were men, before they were metamorphosed by the Great changer, Dokibatl...They also say that when broken into small pieces, and shot into animals, they are sure to cause death." This tradition led Eells to speculate that possibly projectile points had either been made by ancestors of the Indians or had been imported.

He wrote that arrow quivers were made of bear and wolf skins and were by his time very scarce. Shot pouches, especially ornamented ones, were made of skin of the hair seal, of buckskin and cloth. The only defensive armor of which he learned was a shirt or cuirass of dried skin covering the whole body. He used as further proof of the fomer existence of this type of garment the word of an early nineteenth century fur trader, Ross Cox, who had described them as being arrow-proof, remarkably thick, doubled, and thrown over the shoulders with holes for arms, and extending to the ankles. Cox was also Eells' authority for the natives' use of helmets of cedar bark, beargrass and leather, likewise impenetrable by arrows, as well as he was his authority on another kind of armor, "a kind of corset, formed of thin slips of hard wood, ingeniously laced together by bear grass, and much lighter and more pliable than the former, but not covering as much of the body." "I presume," added Eells, "that they depended much more on trees, rocks, and similar natural objects, coupled with a good share of prudence, than upon manufactured articles."

Wilkes was Eells' authority for the use by Skagit Indians of forts of stockades to permit muskets to be fired from these barriers to fend off northern warriors raiding south into Skagit country for slaves. Gibbs was the authority for Eells' description of similar puncheoned fortifications among other peoples of Sound and "Straits." Eells claimed to have seen none of these, "as their wars ceased long ago, and the forts consequently have disappeared."

By contrast, implements for peaceful purposes remained, although as the missionary revealed through his notes and sketches, they had undergone considerable transition. It would appear from his work that some transition had taken place in the implements and techniques used in the working of fibers, although there was resistance to rapid changes. Of spinning tools:

A small one at present used for spinning yarn but formerly used for spinning the material which was used in making blankets and woolen clothes, consists of a circular board or whorl six or seven inches in diameter through the center of which is a stick about two feet long and half an inch in

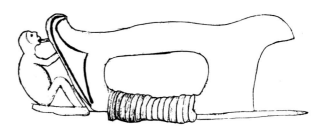

Natives combined both wood and stone to produce implements with which to secure their livelihood. This is hand adze with stone blade used by Klallams.

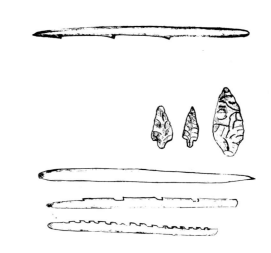

Three upper sketches and lowest are bone duck spear points found near Port Townsend. Between are three stone arrowheads.

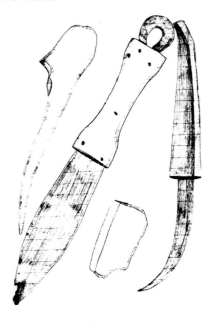

Native-made knives. One on right and one next to left had blades made from old rasps and handles of bone. One on left is all bone, used mainly for cutting open skins and dressing animals. Small item is slate stone knife.

diameter tapering toward each end. The material to be spun is fastened to one end of the stick; the other end is taken in one hand. The wool, which has first been twisted a little by hand, is taken in the other hand, and the wheel is rolled over and over quite rapidly on the thigh, with the hand which holds it. The yarn is not as even as that spun by machinery or even by American spinning wheels and yet it is so good that hundreds of pairs of socks made from it are sold to the whites every year from the Skokomish reservation alone. Occasionally of late tin whorls have been used, made from the covers of tin lard pails. On the Yakima reservation they are sometimes made of leather, but I have never seen such on the Sound. These have held their own with the women against the inventions of the whites as well as most implements. Twenty years ago, the Indian Agent introduced some American spinning wheels among the annuity goods, on the Skokomish reservation. But while a few learned to use them to some extent, they did not seem to care much for them, and they have been broken until hardly one remains and those who used them have very generally returned to the use of their native ones. Within a few months an Indian from the Snohomish [Tulalip] reservation introduced a new kind, which he saw there, and which the Indians can make. It runs with the foot, and seems to be gaining favor...

Of looms:

One was formerly made, which was used in the manufacture of their blankets. I have seen one of them in use by a Clallam woman in making a rug. Two posts about four feet long, six inches wide and half as thick, were sharpened at one end and driven into the ground, as far apart as the length of the article to be woven. Two holes were made in each of these, one towards the upper end, and the other towards the lower in which two bars were inserted thus joining the posts together. The article to be made was fastened to these bars.

From an examination of Eells' notebooks it is evident that the transition rate from native to American implements was varied, that transition, however, was irresistible, for "nearly every kind of tool...now in use by their white neighbors, are also used by the Indians. A large share of their native ones have already gone out of use, and most of the rest will soon belong [to] the past."

Suggested Reading

Olson, Ronald L. *The Quinault Indians and Adze, Canoe, and House Types of the Northwest Coast,* Seattle, 1967.

Taylor, Herbert C. *Anthropological Investigation of the Medicine Creek Tribes, Coast Salish Indians,* II, New York, 1974.

Stone hammer in shape of pestle was still used in Eells' time, although commonly used ones were of American iron and steel.

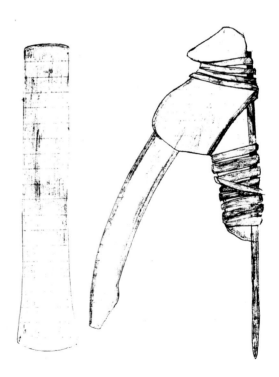

Native-made hand adze in common use. Blade *b,* made from old rasp and hafted with thong *c,* to wooden handle *a.*

Haft of hand adze. This style occasionally found among Klallams, was common among Makahs and Quinaults.

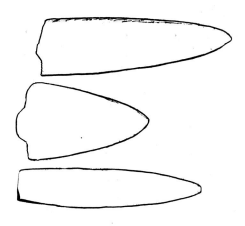

Spearhead from Whatcom County, Wash. Eells, who was familiar with implements from the Columbia River region where items were made of choice stone, believed those made on the Sound to have been poorly fabricated and of poor quality stone.

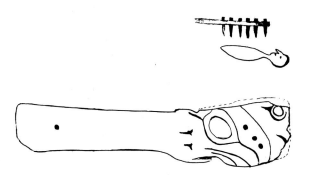

Bone war club found near Dungeness, made of whale rib. Such clubs were also made of wood.

Stone war club. Eells recorded from Indians the story of a group of Tsimshians who, except one woman, were killed by Klallams in the latter's territory in 1868. The United States government put the Klallams in chains and sent the woman to her home in British Columbia with presents, relieving Klallams of having to pay "blood money."

Copper war club. Owner told Eells it was imported from British Columbia and was once worth three slaves in trade.

8: LOCOMOTION AND TRANSPORTATION

In discussing this topic, Eells, as might have been expected, devoted considerable space to methods and means natives used to transport themselves by water. Yet, through his notes he revealed that Puget Sound Indians depended more on land transportation than is popularly believed. Some information he gained in compiling his information was first-hand from journeys he took with Indians between the Skokomish Reservation and the Strait of Juan de Fuca.

On those "Straits," the missionary noted that Klallams had larger canoes and were better navigators than were Indians further up the Sound where there was more protection from ocean winds. Setting the tone for his chapter, he wrote: "Canoes are the friends of the Indians as much as the horse is of the Indian of the prairie or the Arabia, or the sledge of the Eskimo." Of their manufacture:

> In making them they formerly burnt them out, and finished them with the hand adzes of stone, but now they universally use American axes and adzes for the first part of the work and the hand adzes of rasp for the second part, although the finishing touch is put on sometimes with the curved knife. After this they are steamed by filling them with hot water, and throwing in heated stones, to keep it hot, so that they can spread the sides farther apart. They are fastened thus with crosspieces or thwarts which are round or flattened, and an inch and a quarter to two inches in diameter, the size varying with the size of the canoe.
>
> Holes bored through the ends of the cross-pieces and the sides of the canoe admit ropes of cedar which keep the cross-pieces in position. A rim or gunwale is often made for the upper edge of the canoe, about an inch in diameter, which can be replaced when worn out. This is of fir, a harder wood than the cedar of the canoe, as the wear on the rim while paddling is considerable.

Canoes in common use were of three types:

> (1) The large or Chinook canoe...made chiefly by the Indians of British Columbia, and imported ...used very extensively by all the Indians on Puget Sound for carrying large loads and for dangerous travelling, the square stern being said to be a means of safety in rough seas...the largest I have seen among them being 36 feet long, 6 feet wide and 3 feet deep. When travelling with it, it was not hauled up on land, when camping, but anchored as a sloop. The smallest I have seen was eight feet long, but such small ones are not common.

> In travelling in these I have never learned that there was any special place for any person, except in regard to the steersman. Formerly he was a slave. When time with them was worth very little, they preferred to wait for favorable winds. They put a slave to steer, as wind or no wind, he must be at his post.
>
> (2) The shovel canoe, sometimes called the river canoe...These are scarce. They are made in much the same manner, and of about the same size as the next kind, and differ from them mainly in that the ends are from a foot to a foot and a half wide, instead of tapering to a point. They are considered safer in swift rivers.
>
> (3) The fishing or small canoe...These are very common and are entirely of one piece of wood, except that they have the fir rim mentioned as being on the Chinook canoes. They are used for fishing, hunting ducks, travelling on rivers, and even on the Sound when it is calm, and they wish to take only a small load. I have travelled thirty miles in this kind on Hood Canal, though we preferred to keep near shore if possible. Still I have crossed the Canal in one when it was quite rough, and we were in the trough of the sea, for the larger ones withstand considerable waves. In rough water however the Indians are very careful in them. They vary in length from about 12 to 30 feet, in width from 20 to 48 inches, and in depth from nine to 20 inches in the center.

Another canoe type was for racing:

> In 1891 I saw among the Clallams at Elwha, a new kind after the style of American racing canoes, and these were made for this purpose. There were only two of them, each about 30 feet long, and 12 inches deep, one being 26 and the other 28 inches wide. They had not been spread much after being dug out. They were made to be used with oars for four persons, and a rudder.

He observed that sometimes two larger canoes were fastened together side by side and covered with boards to carry large amounts of hay, or to ferry horses for long distances on the Sound. They were not used for crossing rivers, as there were, in his thinking, no rivers in the country so wide that horses could not swim them.

He never knew Puget Sound Indians to use the large Haida canoe, although in his time Haidas often roamed over the lower waters in them. Of their manufacture: "They are made with the stern in much the same shape as the bow, so as better to ride the great waves of the ocean instead of being square at the stern as the Chinook canoe." "It seems," he added, "a little strange that these

Indians should not procure them occasionally, since they are so well adapted to rough waters, and the lower Clallam waters are about as rough as the ocean, and since they import Chinook canoes from other tribes of British Columbia, but so it is that far as a Haida canoe is seen, so far it is known that no Puget Sound Indians are in it. Even the Makahs and Quinaielt Indians, on the ocean shores do not use them, and I do not know that any tribes of the Selish family do.

Although many Indians owned boats of American make, such craft had not replaced canoes as much as had most other articles of "civilized manufacture," those of native origin:

> The reason…[was that] most Indians do not see the superiority of our boats. They are heavier, generally travel slower, and the person propelling sits looking backward and continually twists his head around to see where he is going. The canoe is light, and one person often travels as fast in one with one paddle, as the white man does with two oars. He looks forward and sees where he is going and all the snags. True we think the boat is safer, with its keel, but the Indian, accustomed to his canoe from infancy, feels as safe in it as we do in our boats. In fact considering the amount the Indians are on the water, they meet with far less accidents than the white man does.

Eells knew of but one Indian who could make a good boat, and he was raised by a step-father, a white man who had learned the occupation by carefully observing techniques used in a nearby shipyard. Very few Indians had procured sloops for which there was but little business since steamers had rendered such craft unprofitable for both Indians and whites.

Among paddle types which he catalogued was the "common man's paddle," most generally used on the Sound, of maple and about four and a half feet long. Another was the woman's paddle of the same material, a little shorter and a little broader in the blade. Another was the "Makah paddle" imported from that people and used considerably by Klallams and Indians further up the Sound. Commonly of yew, larger ones were some five feet long, with blades three feet long and seven inches wide. Once in a while, as Eells recorded, Haida paddles were seen among Klallams. Large ones were five and a half feet long, with blades three and a third feet by six inches wide. Some of these were "very fancifully painted, with the eye of the thunder bird and the like, though I do not remember ever having seen one such in use. They evidently are thus painted to sell." The "Chehalis or river paddle" differed from other types by having blade ends cut out, leaving them somewhat "U"-shaped. They were used on log-filled rivers since ends of the paddles, when fitted on logs, enabled rowers to push their craft away from such

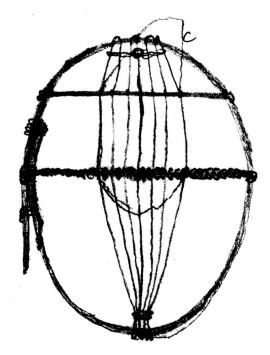

Snowshoes were little used except in winter hunting in mountains. An oblong or oval rim of hazelwood was laced with thongs. The heel fitted near the center and toes extended to the front *c*. Shoe was fastened to foot by means of thongs.

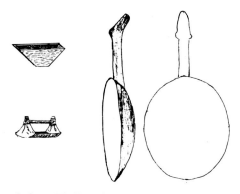

Above left, a Klallam bailer without handle. On bottom of bailer was groove for grasping. Below left, is Klallam bailer made of cedar bark bent up at ends and gathered and fastened by stick between ends to make a handle. Not strong, these were not used much.
On right, oval, shallow Twana dipper with carved handle.

Pointed Twana paddle above made of maple. Preferred yew wood was scarce. Paddles were about 4½-foot long, slightly longer for men, and wider at the blade for women. Made of yew wood they were only about 5 feet long.

obstacles. They did not, however, cut the water as well as did other types.

Of oars, Eells noted that the Indians had known nothing until whites came, but used them considerably on larger canoes by his time. On larger canoes sails were used, the largest craft having two, the smallest, none. "Formerly the cedar bark mat was used, but they have now gone entirely out of date, and those of cloth fashioned and fastened after the style of those in our skiffs are used. Many a sail has been made entirely of flour sacks, and the flour brands on them in various shapes, often are very comical."

Other navigational aids which he described were ten or fifteen-foot poles used for travelling against strong winds especially around land points, and in ascending swift shallow streams. Although some Indians had adopted white men's rudders to their large canoes, most preferred the old way of steering with a paddle. Usually the best paddlers were selected according to circumstance: "If the water is rough the strongest and most experienced navigator steers, but if the rowing is hard, and the steering easy, the strongest person rows, and perhaps a boy or woman steers. I have more than once been in canoes, sailing when the wind was so strong, that it required two persons, with oars to steer."

Formerly of stone, most anchors of Eells' time were of some kind of old iron. He described native bailing vessels for canoes as being of three types: of wood from five to seven inches long exclusive of the handle, and variations of this; of wood without a handle, usually about ten inches by six and two and a half inches deep; and finally, of cedar bark, not too widely used.

Of trade goods (not all of which was waterborne):

> They have dishes made from the horn of the mountain sheep, which are said to have come from the Stikine Indians of British Columbia, six or eight hundred miles to the north; the dentalia shell, their ancient money also came from the same region. They occasionally obtain articles from the Haida Indians of Queen Charlottes Island. They get pipes, horn dishes, buffalo robes and baskets from the Klikitats and Yakimas of Eastern Washington, one or two hundred miles to the east; baskets from the Cowlitz Indians, a hundred miles to the south, and from the Shoalwater Bay and Quinaielt Indians on the coast, about the same distance to the west and southwest. The distance mentioned is nearly in a direct line, the way in which the articles come is much farther, sometimes twice as far. The northern commerce is mainly by water, but that with the Klikitat, Yakima, Cowlitz, Shoalwater Bay and Quinaielt Indians, by land, which accounts for the difference in the distance...The articles from these distant tribes is, however limited in number, and many of them are obtained through intermediate tribes,

Travel among native peoples led to exchange of products passing from one group to another. Top, an imported Makah basket of small round split twigs. Below, an imported fancy Makah table basket. According to Eells, Makahs fabricated "the best made" baskets, often with covers. These were used by native Puget Sound women to hold sewing materials.

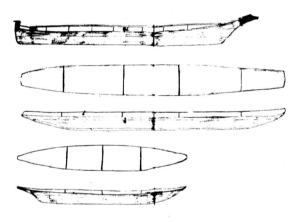

Upper canoe is called "Chinook canoe," although made by natives to the north in British Columbia and imported by natives to the south. It cost $100.00 in Eells' time. This 35-foot craft with square stern for safe travel in rough water had a separately carved, projecting bow piece. There were two places to fit masts near middle and at bow. Eells wrote that a 60-foot Chinook canoe was exhibited at the Centennial Exhibition in Philadelphia in 1876.

Canoe at center, seen both from top and side, is a "shovel nose" river craft with blunted ends. Scarce when Eells was there, it was of one piece.

Bottom canoe, seen also from side and from top, was common fishing and small river canoe. It was of one piece except for its fir rim. It was used for travel on the Sound only on calm days. Varying from 12 to 30 feet this type was not pulled upon the shore as were Chinook canoes when not in use. Instead, it was anchored in the water.

Haida paddle, top, had wider handles than most others and ends were less pointed.
Bottom, a Chehalis paddle with end cut out to make it useful for river travel where there were many floating logs to push out of the way.

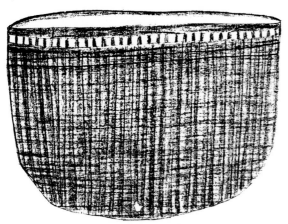

Diamond-shaped canoe bailer with handle. This type was made of alder, maple or laurel and was usually 5 to 7 inches wide across the middle.

Travel brought many products from other areas to the Sound. This is a cedar bark basket Klallams imported from British Columbia Indians.

A flexible grass bag imported by a Twana from the Klickitats.

who serve as carriers. The great bulk of trade was between the tribes who surrounded Puget Sound, in the United States and British Columbia. These often met at potlatches, and quite an extensive trade was carried on.

Under a section entitled "Trips," Eells narrated two journeys he took from the Skokomish Reservation to Dungeness on the Strait of Juan de Fuca. On an 1876 journey, traveling time from the former to the latter place had been a fast twenty-three summertime hours, yet a much slower pace than the "eight miles per hour" he had once experienced when traveling in an Indian canoe. On a wintertime 1878 journey between the two points he joined some sixty-five Twanas in seven canoes to attend a potlatch. Inclement weather, common at that season, forced the women and children passengers to squat under canoe-length protective matting. "It was rather comical," he mused, "to see a number of persons, mostly women and children, sitting in a canoe with a mat stretched over them, extending almost from one end of the canoe to the other." Delaying the journey, besides inclement weather, was a stop to raise the canoe on blocks so that a pitch-wood fire could be applied to its underside to burn off mosses or other accumulations so that it could glide through the water more easily. Stops were made to "tamanous" for fair winds. "In addition to the tamanous for wind..." wrote Eells, "they would, especially in a calm, when they wished for a fair wind, pound on the canoe with their paddles or strike the water with them, spattering it foreward." They often whistled for wind. A two-hour delay at Port Townsend gave the Indians opportunity to purchase presents for the principle men at the potlatch. The entire journey consumed but twenty-two traveling hours, with the return journey taking some ten hours longer.

Of pedestrian travel:

They generally travel only short distances on foot, seldom more than 10 miles, except in hunting. In coming to the Twana potlatch of 1878, however, the Quinaielt Indians came about 100 miles, much of it on foot. There was too much land travel to allow them to come entirely by land, and too much water travel to admit bringing horses. So they brought their canoes as far as they could, and walked the rest of the way...In their short journeys they often, the women especially, carry large loads. The way they usually prefer to do this is to take the carrying strap, tie the ends, which are several feet long, around the load, when it is of wood, mats, and such articles, or into the handles of baskets filled with potatoes, fish, apples, and other small objects. They then place the load on the back, and the flat part of the strap around the forehead. Formerly these straps were made of some tough bark, such as that of alder, braided. Now they use straps woven of strings and rags.

This strap is from a foot to a foot and a half long, and two or three inches wide, with ropes at each end perhaps five feet long...

For winter travel, he noted that snowshoes were scarce and little used except for winter hunting in the mountains. These shoes, as Eells described them, were commonly oblong, oval, about 14 by 18 inches with a hazelwood rim, across which thongs of dried hides were passed.

Among means of travel by land by Eells' time were horses, which he observed were used more by Twanas and other tribes up the Sound than by Klallams, since the land of the latter was mountainous, separating them from lands of other peoples. Because of the heavily forested areas of the Sound region and its poor roads, horses, wrote Eells, were never in great use before the coming of white men: "Hence, they took very little pride in adorning their saddles and horses with trappings [as did Indians east of the Cascade Mountains]" Since the country had been settled, he thought the Indians had adopted saddles used by whites which also had no special trappings. He believed horses were introduced to the Sound by Indians east of the Cascade Mountains. To deduce that they were so introduced, he used his knowledge of native languages especially by making a comparative study of various native words for "horse."

He believed sleds were almost the only vehicles used by Twanas and Klallams when he came among them in 1874. In fact, he remembered that the government had no wagons on the Skokomish Reservation, their only wheeled vehicles being heavy carts. Soon after, however, the Indians introduced wagons and buggies onto reservations. The Puyallups, he believed, had more and better ones than others because of the proximity of these people to the city of Tacoma, and because of their wealth.

Under a section entitled "Travels," he noted that some typical travel patterns were

mainly among the tribes among which they intermarried. All of the tribes bordering the Sound had more or less intercourse with each other, owing to the ease with which they could travel the waters of the Sound, which lay between them. In addition the Clallams visited the Makahs, Quillehutes, and tribes bordering the Straits of Fuca in British Columbia. The Skokomish Indians went to the Chehalis and Quinaielts. The Chehalis travelled to the Quinaielt, Cowlitz and Chinook region, and sometimes went to the Columbia river, and Willamette valley. The Nisqually and Puyallup Indians went south likewise to the Columbia, and east, across the Cascades to the Klikitat and Yakima country. In fact after the Indians were conquered in the war of 1855-6, the chiefs fled to that region. The Duwamish and Snohomish Indians likewise went east, while the Skagits and

End of dish made of horn of mountain sheep, as reported by Eells. This type dish was imported by Sound Indians on travels east to Cascade Mountains and north to British Columbia.

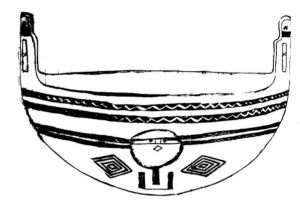

Figure shows incised design from side view of horn dish above.

Lummis travelled north to the tribes of British Columbia.

Other travels, which Eells noted, took Indians from their native haunts. The Duke of York, a Klallam chief, and a few other Klallams went aboard ship to San Francisco, and a John Palmer went from that city to the mouth of the Amur River on the eastern Pacific. A large number of children were taken for schooling to Forest Grove and Chemawa in Oregon, and some had been to schools in the East.

As Indians also traveled to gain their livelihood in an economy increasingly dominated by white men, they also found time for games and pastimes which had undergone some changes with the advent of white men. Eells next discussed these diversions in his notes.

Suggested Reading

Olson, Ronald L. *The Quinault Indians and Adze, Canoe, and House Types of the Northwest Coast,* Seattle, 1967.

Suttles, P. Wayne. *The Economic Life of the Coast Salish of Haro and Rosario Straits, Coast Salish Indians, I,* New York, 1974.

9: GAMES AND PASTIMES

In this chapter Eells matched his description of Indian games, especially intricate ones involving gambling, with sketches of the paraphernalia used in such gaming. It was his practice when discussing various aspects of Indian life to insert observations of other white men. He did this in this topic with a lengthy description by a newspaper correspondent of an Indian gambling game in 1894. As in other topics, this one revealed the impact of white culture on that of the Indian.

It was evident to the missionary that gambling had for ages been an important activity among the natives:

> They have a tradition that a long time ago a great supernatural being called Do-ki batl came here and told them to give up all bad habits; these [gambling] disks being among the things that they were to give up. He took the disks and threw them into the water, but they came back; he then took them and threw them into the fire, but they came out; he threw them away as far as he could, but again they came back; and so he threw them away five times, and every time they returned; and so, as they conquered him, he told the Indians that they might retain this kind of gambling for fun and sport.

Gambling, he observed, had been very common, "there having been but very few who did not engage in it, and even now are by no means wholly free from it." As in the white community, professional gamblers plied their trade, often visiting large gatherings, especially potlatches. He noted, too, that gambling was not as common among women as it was among men. One game was played with round disks:

> This is a men's game generally, though sometimes both sexes engage in it. The disks are about two inches in diameter and a third of an inch thick. They are made of hard wood, quite smooth, and by long continued use become highly polished. The edge of most of them is partly painted, either red or black, while one is left unpainted, or else the edge is entirely painted. There are ten blocks or disks in a set.
> Cedar bark is beaten up fine and the disks are divided into handsful of five each, and each handful is then placed under some of the cedar bark on a mat, while the players face each other, But two persons engage at the same time in shuffling the disks, though others are generally around and bet on it, and one of them occasionally changes with one of the players, if his friend should be unlucky. A number of small sticks about four inches long are placed on a board for a tally. At first they are evenly divided, but are changed as one party wins

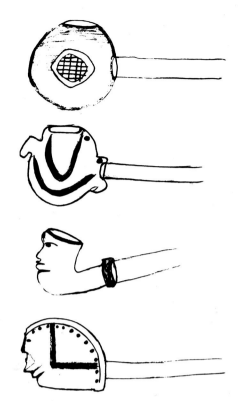

In Eells years on the Sound, American pipes were in common use. Native pipes were also used. All of these soft clay stone pipes were made by Klallams except that next to the bottom, made by a Makah. All were intended to be used with wooden stems.

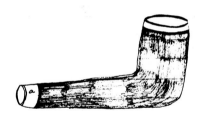

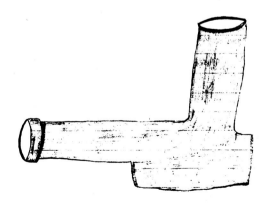

Smoking was pastime Sound natives rarely indulged in before whites lived among them. These are soft clay stone pipes; upper, made by a Yakima Indian, but used by a Twana; lower, made by a Twana.

or loses. The object is for one party or persons to win them all. Usually from twelve to twenty-four of these sticks are used; the number used depending on the amount of the bet. As one party may win and lose, and continue to do so, it is plain that the game may last a long time, for four days and nights and then be a draw game.

When all is ready for the game, the parties sit down on the ground about twelve feet from each other, and one selects one out of his half a dozen or more sets and shuffles them around considerably; then, under cover, divides them evenly so that five are in each hand and places each handful under some of this cedar bark. They are then shuffled around on the mats for a time, the opposite player watching all this as closely as possible. His wish is to guess under which hand the disk is which has the painted rim or the unpainted one. With a motion of his hand he indicates under which hand he thinks this one to be, and the player rolls them out. If he guesses aright he wins and plays next; but if he guesses wrong he loses, and the other plays again. They have several sets of these blocks, so that, if bad luck attends one set for a time, they may change to and use another set.

These different sets are marked a little differently on the sides, or else are made slightly different in size to distinguish them, all of each set being alike. They are usually about two inches in diameter and a quarter of an inch thick.

Eells cited another form of this game, called the "tamahnous game." As he described it, a large number of people, including women, who had a tamanous, participated, but only the men shuffled the disks. Sometimes the contest was intertribal in nature. The basic difference between this game and the one previously described was that participants invoked the aid of their tamanous. Wrote the missionary:

> While one man plays, another member of his party beats the drum or tomtom, or possibly two of these are used, and the rest of the party clap their hands and sing, each one as I am told singing his or her tamahnous song, to invoke the aid of his or her special guardian spirit. There is certainly no uniformity in their songs, as different persons sing different songs at the same time."

Seldom did they play for the mere love of mere fun, but for the love of money with stakes ranging on occasion up to four hundred or even a thousand dollars and "even to clothes on their backs," with outside parties, like white men, betting on the games.

Another native game was played with bones. In this contest

> A small bone about two inches long and a half inch in diameter is used, or sometimes two of them, one of which is marked. They also at times use two

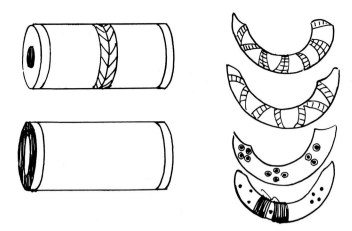

Muskrat teeth used in gambling by women. They are marked on but one side.

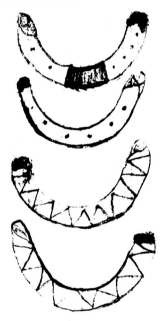

Above, marked beaver teeth much used as dice for women's gambling. Below, bone gambling sticks used by both women and men. Used in pairs, one was marked for a guessing game to determine which hand held the marked bone.

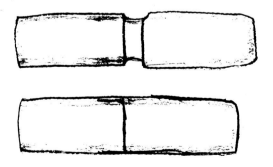

Brass gambling implements fabricated so as to be used for cheating.

Below is a two-inch gambling disc made of polished hardwood. Above, is a stack of them. The writing is Eell's.

Bows were used by children as playthings in Eells' time on Puget Sound. They were used as war weapons during the mid-1880s.

Rectangular rattle with hole through it to serve as handle. It was put together with wooden pegs, then painted and used at great festivals to call people together.

much larger ones, two and a half inches long and an inch or more in diameter, one of which is marked. Occasionally also pieces of wood of the same size are used, but they are considered a poor affair.

Six or eight persons on each side usually play this game, but more may be really engaged in it on the outside, and even the whole tribe, as in the previous game. The drum and the tamahnous are also occasionally used. The players sit in two rows opposite each other, about six feet apart. In front of each set of players is a long stick or rail, and each of them except one have small sticks about a foot and a half long, with which, while the one on their side in playing, they pound on the rail, singing at the same time to induce good luck. The one who has no stick in his hands takes the bone or bones in his hands, under cover either of a blanket or some such thing, arranges which shall be in each hand, if both are used, or in which hand it shall be if one is used, and then in sight very rapidly changes them from hand to hand. This is done so quickly, by long practice, that the bones cannot be seen. After a time one of the opposite players by a motion indicates in which hand he thinks the bone is, if one is used, or, if two are used, in which hand the marked one is. If he guesses aright, he wins and plays; if not, he loses and the other one continues to play...

The tally is kept with striped sticks about a foot long, which are stuck into the ground, but on the same principle as the previous game. I have known a game to be played for four days and nights, and neither party to win, it being a draw game. If one person on a side is peculiarly successful, he will play for a long time; but if he is very unsuccessful, another of his party will take the bones.

Eells observed that bets in this game were sometimes small—pins and matches, fifty cents or a dollar and a half. Sometimes the stakes, he noted, were much larger.

Yet another game was the "women's game":

Beavers' teeth are usually used for this, though sometimes those of muskrats. Commonly only one person on each side plays, but sometimes there are two or three. The teeth are marked on one side so as to form two pairs of two each, one of them having a string tied around it. They are all taken in one hand and thrown up, and the manner in which they fall shows how the game goes; it being somewhat on the principle of throwing dice. If the marked side of the one which has the string on it is down and all the rest up, or up while the rest are down, it counts four; if that side of all is up or down, it counts two. If the marked side of one pair is up, and that of the other pair down, it counts one and if the pair one of which has the string on it is up or down and the other pair is divided, it counts nothing. To get thirty is a game, but generally they play three games and bet money, dresses, cloth and the like. The women sometimes learn to throw them very expertly, although quickly by holding the one with the string on it a trifle longer than the others, and then give it a peculiar turn so as to make it fall differently from them.

They usually keep tally with small sticks about four inches long, but, if they can, they use the bones of birds of about the same length. But the women play this game very little, as compared with the time devoted by the men to the other games.

The lengthy article which Eells incorporated in his notes appeared in the February 11, 1894 issue of the *Seattle Post Intelligencer*. It described a "sing-gamble" game played at Renton, near Seattle, pitting "Black and Cedar River [Duwamish] Indians" against the Puyallups. The contest was a marathon affair dragging out for a period of four days and nights, after which the players were completely exhausted and the game declared a draw. The article was very informative, but in contrast to Eells' scholarly approach in recording Indian culture, its author used the humorous, Indian denigrating style so popular in his day.

Gambling games, which Indians learned from white men, were played with cards. "It is," the missionary half chided, "about the only kind of civilized (!) gambling which they have learned, with a few exceptions." A few Indians took up white men's style dancing, although many continued to dance in a style more Indian than white. In this dance type no partners were chosen,

> but both men and women dance; the men holding on to each other's hands by themselves and the women doing the same, though all in the same room. White people would hardly call it dancing, for it is simply a jumping up and down, sometimes in the same place and sometimes all move along together, in the house and out of it, while they keep time to the drum and singing. Generally this dancing is a religious performance, a part of their tamahnous, but occasionally it is practiced for mere sport. I have seen them do so until they were entirely exhausted by their laughing and sports.

Of another pastime, horse racing, as far as Eells knew,

> the Clallams have very little of any of this, as their horses are few. At least they have no race track. The other tribes mentioned have practiced it largely for many years, as their outdoor summer sport, the gambling having been their indoor

winter sport. They do not do as much of it now by any means as they did twenty years ago, still at times, especially at their Fourth of July celebrations, and hop-picking, they have large races, sometimes one tribe being against another. As far as they can, they usually practice it, as the whites do, without a book of rules.

Some of the old games like arrow shooting to determine who could shoot the greatest distance, and on which bets were placed, were entirely out of style. Newer sports, borrowed from the white community, became popular with younger people. Such a game was baseball in which the youngsters, as they played, chattered in English throughout the contests. Of another youthful game:

> In imitating whites they sometimes have several post-offices a short distance from each other, with as many postmasters, and a mail carrier who carries bits of paper from one to the other, or they will hold a council in remembrance of the time when some distinguished person from Washington has been here, when they will make speeches, have an interpreter, and all things in regular order. Again it will occasionally be a church, while they go through with the services, or a court with judge, jury, lawyers, witnesses, and a criminal. An odd occurrence took place at one of these mock courts some time ago which happened to be overheard by their teacher. A boy was on trial for drunkenness. When the proper time came the criminal arose and said substantially as follows: 'Gentlemen, I am a poor man and not able to employ a lawyer, so I must plead my own case. The court has been slightly mistaken about the case. I am a white man; my name is Captain Chase (a white man living near the [Skokomish] reservation). I came to church on Sunday. The minister did not know me; as I was well dressed he thought I was a good man, and might have something to say, hence he asked me to speak. I knew I was not a suitable man to address the congregation, but I could not well refuse. So I rose and went to the platform, but I had some tobacco in my mouth. I tried quietly to take it out, and throw it down without being seen, but the Indians noticed it, and thought a minister should not chew tobacco, and beside I did stagger a little. These are the reasons I am on trial here.'

Suggested Reading

Elmendorf, W. W. *The Structure of Twana Culture, Research Studies, Washington State University,* XXVIII, 3, Pullman, Washington, 1960.

10: ART AND MUSIC

In his discussion of art, Eells appeared, subtly at least, to have advanced two ideas; firstly, that the art of Puget Sound Indians, although not as highly advanced as that of their northern neighbors of British Columbia, did have considerable merit on its own; and secondly, that a great deal of it found its way onto objects of utilitarian nature. Although it might be said that he did not specifically wish to reveal that the natives' music was as diverse as their art, it is obvious to the reader of the notes that it was. Although he did not discuss native art as a critic, he came close to being one when discussing native music, for as a missionary, among whose working tools were his Christian songs, he gave the impression that native songs of greatest merit were those rendered as much as possible in the harmonics and homiletics of the Christian faith.

Prefacing his discussion of art, Eells wrote:

There is no special class of artists among them as there is among the tribes to the north in British Columbia, still they make considerable work that is quite artistic on baskets, cloth, leather, wood, etc.

Their work as a general thing does not equal that of more northern tribes, but is fully equal to that of tribes east and south.

Little however is wasted on the desert air, or made merely for ornament, but it is generally put upon some useful article.

Useful articles upon which natives revealed their artistry were baskets, the sketching of which gave Eells opportunity to reveal his own artistry, especially when sketching those which incorporated colored grass in a variety of figures and designs. Grass work, which made for beautiful baskets, was also applied to other articles: "The Clallams and tribes farther up the Sound import bottles made by the Makahs and Quinaielts, bottles of various sizes, from vials to quart junk bottles, covered with fine grass work, which are beautifully figured ... These are covered simply for the beauty of it, or for sale."

He revealed that native artistry also appeared on cloth as well as on glass: "The straps, with which they carry their baskets and other loads, are ornamented by weaving different colored cloth strings into the strap, as it is made...These are common to all the tribes on the Sound, and might be largely multiplied." He noted that fancy rugs were also covered with woven figures of such objects as dogs, chickens, deer, trees and some soldiers. Shot pouches, some of which were imported from British Columbia, were covered sometimes with beadwork. Of beads: "It is said

On Left, detail of incised work from horn dish on page 48. On right, imported horn spoon with carving.

Eells copied incised figures made by a Klallam on a stone hammer. Uppermost two represented bird's head, side and top view; below it, a deer, fish, birds, and a dog.

Horn spoon with carved handle imported by a Twana from Quinaults. Beside it, a bone shawl pin, seen in two views to show the carving.

that formerly after the whites first came, they ornamented with beads to a great extent, but of late the art is almost entirely neglected." Of artwork on other articles: "Pin cushions of patch work ...and patch work quilts, some of which are very artistic, are becoming common. I have seen a pin cushion made by an Indian girl, between the sides of a clam shell, which was well done. In mittens they often knit figures, though they are rarely of any significance . . ."

Occupying considerable space in Eells' discussion of native art was that pertaining to carvings and paintings on wood, and often done, he opined, "for mere amusement." Occasionally," he explained, "they carve a person in wood for mere ornament. One woman at Skokomish has owned the wooden figure of a man...carved, about twelve inches long, and of proportionate size, dressed in white's clothes. Her sister had its companion, a woman ... dressed like a white woman. These were carved by their father, a Port Madison Indian." Continued Eells:

A Clallam carved for me a man, about nine inches long and dressed as they sometimes do, when performing at their potlatches. He has on very little clothing. The face below the nose, the upper part of the chest, and the hair are painted red. The latter is done up in a knot which projects in front. He holds in his hands across his stomach a carved face...A Twana man carved for me a small man, six inches long, dressed as Americans do. The same person also prepared for me the face and chest of a man. The face is about eight inches long by seven wide and is a natural growth on a maple tree. It looked very much like an old Indian, so much so that he said he would fix it up for me if I wished, so he smoothed the face, a very little, put some brass headed nails in the eyes and nose, earrings in the ears, and put on a small body...

One canoe, formerly owned by a Twana, had on its head, a carved figure supposed to be a monkey, in bas-relief, the joint of the fore-leg being raised one and a quarter inches, and that of the hind leg two inches, but the middle of the body is in very low relief.

Of carving on houses:

A Clallam chief at Elwha, Cultus John, had a few years ago two large side posts in his house, two or two and a half feet wide, and six or eight inches thick, each carved so as to represent a large man, one of whom held a frog in his hands. The work was excellently done by a regular carver of the Nittinat tribe of British Columbia. On account of the death of his son, the chief destroyed his house, but moved the posts to the grave, where they remained a few years. The last time however I vis-

Figures worked into flexible baskets with aniline dyed grass. Largest on right was imported from Chehalis Indians; other two baskets are Twana-made. Designs around top of Chehalis basket represented dogs.

Music scores made by Eells.

ited the place, the chief had died, and the posts were gone. When he set them in the ground at the grave, he put them in nearly to the elbows…

Besides the representation on the post of a man clasping a frog to his stomach, there was a carving on yet another post representing a woman. Masks nailed on the side of the forehead of one of these human figures was in imitation of the face and head of a jug; another mask portrayed a bird, while yet another of these face coverings which opened and shut, was divided, one half being nailed on the side of the forehead of each figure.

From the notes one learns that wooden dishes were sometimes ornamented with carved figures, sometimes the thunderbird, and, that carvings were also done on horn dishes which Twanas imported from British Columbia natives and from the Klickitats east of the Cascade Mountains. Eells obtained such a carved spoon from a Twana Indian who had gotten it in some manner from the Quinaults. And of course, war implements as clubs were ornamented, particularly with the thunderbird, which symbol, noted Eells, also appeared on more peaceful objects as gambling pieces, metal pin heads and bracelets, the latter imported from Makahs and British Columbia natives. Carvings, of which the missionary had heard, or had in his collection, also appeared on objects of stone and clay.

Turning from art to another basic form of native culture, music, he believed that it consisted

more of noise than melody. As a rule the Klallams are far more musical than the Twanas. The women sometimes sing alone when at work, at funerals, and when tending the children; but in nearly all their gambling, war, boat, and religious songs the men take the lead, the women however joining. Usually all persons sing the same melody, though sometimes the pitch varies considerably. At some of the tamahnous ceremonies, I have heard nearly all singing a different song, each one as I have been told sing his or her tamahnous song. At a distance of a few hundred yards, however, all of these seemed to blend into one harmony.

He found instruments fitting to accompany the songs: "These are intended more for noise than anything else. Indeed, no single one can vary the tone, the only modifications being loud and soft. They are used chiefly in their religious performances…They consist of the drum, deer-hoof rattles, scallop shell rattles, and hollow rattles made from wood. Those who have no instruments pound with small sticks on larger ones, and clap their hands."

He knew of instruments used only to accompany war, gambling, boat, and religious songs, in all of which natives invoked their tamanous, making them in reality, he believed, religious songs "continually repeated."

Of boat songs to which he alluded:

> When travelling in a common way they are not accustomed to sing much, but sometimes when on a parade before friends, generally on the arrival of several canoes at a council or great festival, there is considerable singing, accompanied by humming, clapping of hands, pounding with stick and paddles, on boards and canoes, and sometimes by rattling with the hollow, wooden rattles. This occurs just before the landing, beginning sometimes when the canoes are two or three miles away, as far as they can easily be heard.

Eells heard one of these songs in 1875 when Klallams of Elwha arrived at a council at Dungeness, and heard one again in 1878 when these same Indians arrived at the same place to attend another potlatch.

Another type of song which he heard was that of a patriotic nature. He tells how at one time

> in traveling with a large number of Twana Indians, one of whom was a Chemakum woman [of one of the Twana bands which according to tradition, as Eells recorded it, was driven by a high tide from Quinault country to occupy lands from the mouth of Hood Canal to the mouth of Port Discovery Bay], whose husband was a Twana, we passed through the Chemakum country. When we reached it, she began singing something, but at first I did not understand what she was doing. I asked the other Indians about it, and they said 'Hush.' I did so as they all kept still. They afterwards told me that she was singing an ode in the Chemakum language to her native land. None of them understood her, but out of respect to her they kept silent. This has been the only song of the kind I have ever heard.

In certain types of gambling, Eells, as noted above, found singing very common, accompanied by the pounding on large sticks with smaller ones, as different songs were sung by contesting parties. He saw no meaning in the words. In other types of gambling he knew of no singing unless the contest became a tamanous game

> when a drum, one for each party, is brought in, and there is pounding on sticks and clapping of hands and singing. In this singing each person sings his or her tamahnous song, thus invoking the aid of his or her tamanous, so as to win the game. I was once present at such game and when in the house the singing was a confused medly on different keys and I could catch nothing of it, but when I was a few hundred yards away the sound had mainly blended ... though different keys mainly in chord were distinguished.

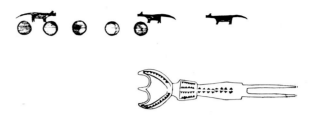

Below, carving done on handle of fish spear. The above design was on a house board found at Dungeness with moons and cats carved on it.

Carving on wooden dish representing thunderbird was imported by Klallam Indian from British Columbia.

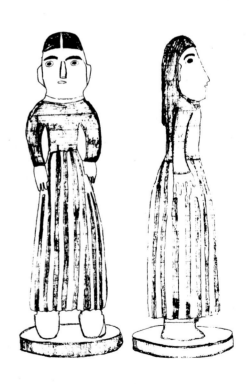

Front and side views of carving of woman in white woman's dress.

Universality of their songs was seen in those ranging from nursery tunes to soothe crying children or to hush them to sleep, to those sung at funerals and during other periods of mourning:

At all funerals, and often for several days afterwards, there is a crying kind of singing, with no accompaniment. Generally however all do not sing the same melody at the same time in unison. One may sing alone, or several may sing at the same time, and perhaps the same melody, but perhaps each will begin and finish as he or she may wish, paying no attention to any of the rest. Often for weeks or even months, after an especially dear friend has died, some one, almost universally a woman, will sit near her house, and cry or sing by the hour. At the funerals usually both men and women sing...

Eells had heard war songs only rarely "as wars have ceased, long ago," and then only at some great festival as a potlatch in memory of former days. In contrast to these songs, he found religious ones "almost universal." These, he observed, were sung to seek fair winds for a journey, accompanied by the beating of a drum and pounding on sticks. They were also sung when medicine men attempted to cure sick patients. At black tamanous ceremonies a song was "universally begun by a leader, then another person took it up, the first one stopping, then all, from twenty to forty persons, joined in it, with a small drum, and hollow wooden rattles, and lastly the large drum was used. The song was repeated several times, and it ended with a great 'hi' or 'ho,' meaning 'done'..."

He was unable to obtain work or love songs.

In attempting to introduce Christian music among the Indians he found it difficult to translate "our hymns" into the Chinook jargon [a lingua franca devised in white fur trading days], or to compose any that would rhyme, forcing him "to teach some truth that can be sung to one of our tunes." In 1878 he prepared a small Chinook jargon hymnbook which was copyrighted and published by a man in Portland, Oregon. In the introduction to a second and enlarged edition published in 1889, he wrote:

These hymns have grown out of Christian work among the Indians. They repeat often, because they are intended chiefly for Indians who cannot read, and hence must memorize them; but as soon as they learn to read, they sing in English. It will be noticed that often two syllables must be sung to one note. The chief peculiarity which I have noticed in making hymns in this language is, that a large proportion of the words are two syllables, and a large majority of these have the accent on the second syllable, which renders it almost impossible to compose any hymns in long, common or short metres.

With Indian help, the missionary also prepared a few songs in the Twana, (which he characterized as a difficult language), Klallam and Nisqualli languages, and one in the Snohomish dialect of the Nisqualli taken from a prayer book and catechism of that language by the Reverend J.B. Brouillet, a Roman Catholic priest on the Snohomish Reservation. One jargon hymn in the notebooks, but not published in the hymnbook went as follows:

1. Saghalie Tyee, yaka mamook
   Konoway illahee, konoway kah
      (Repeat both lines.)
   Chorus Yaka mamook, yaka mamook
      Konoway illahee, konoway kah.

2. Saghalie Tyee, yaka mamook
   Konoway tillikums, konoway kah
      (Repeat both lines.)
      Yaka mamook, yaka mamook
      Konoway tillikums, konoway kah.

Translation

1. God made
   All the earth, Everywhere.
   He made, he made,
   All the earth, Everywhere.

2. God made
   All the people, Everywhere.
   He made, he made,
   All the people Everywhere.

Other verses satisfying both the Indians' love of repetition and Eells' theology were made by changing the second word in the second and fourth lines to *iktas*, "things"; *muckamuck*, "food"; *moosmoos*, "cattle"; *kuitan*, "horses"; *tupso*, "grass," etc.

Eells demonstrated the Indians' love of repetition in their singing by including in his notes a Twana hymn, from a tune, "The Hebrew Children," in which the name "Noah" in the first line could be substituted by others as "Moses," "Daniel," "Jesus," or as many others as Eells was able to provide, and the Indians, inclined to sing. He supplied Klallams a hymn in their own language to the popular tune of his day, "John Brown."

Suggested Reading

Gunther, Erna. *Art in the Life of the Northwest Coast Indian,* Portland, 1966.
Holm, Bill. *Northwest Coast Indian Art,* Seattle, 1965.

11: FUNERAL CUSTOMS

In this chapter Eells described the natives' customs attending the disposal of their dead, explaining to some extent the motivations and beliefs of those who observed them. In his sketches he portrayed the many material elements involved in the burial of the dead.

On native burials, Eells wrote: "They generally bury much sooner after death than the whites, about as soon as they can after obtaining the coffin. They have sometimes been so much in haste as to ask the government carpenter to make the coffin before death had actually taken place, and in one or two instances they actually began making the grave clothes for a person, while alive, who recovered." Formerly "they were very superstitious about going near the dead, and hence it was difficult to induce them to attend Christian services at a funeral. They feared that the evil spirit which killed the deceased, was hovering around, and would enter and kill the living also. They were more especially afraid to have children approach a corpse, as they believed them to be more likely to be killed by the evil spirit, than a grown person." The "superstitious fear" spirit which had killed the deceased, still hovered in the house where death had occurred:

For this reason they often built a house of mats near by, into which they removed a sick person, just before death, so that it should be torn down after the death, when the spirit would leave. If a person died in a good, permanent house too good to be torn down, the survivors would desert the house, and perhaps tear off the roof, nor would they return to live in it for from one to three years. As they became more civilized I have noticed some singular changes in the superstitions. One has been that the living must not pass out the door, through which the dead was carried out. Hence in one case, when a Twana child died in a good house, I saw the dead carried out of the window, the family afterwards living in the house. At another time a dead person had been carried out through the only door in the house, the door was taken down, and removed to the other end of the house, and the old doorway was permanently closed, the family continuing to live in the house. Then as the Indians learned that the whites had disenfectant medicines, they have believed such to be a sufficient remedy for the evil spirits, and have obtained carbolic acid to scatter around in the house, although the disease of which the deceased died, might not have been in the least degree contagious.

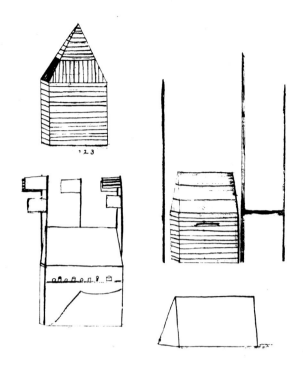

Klallam burials. Above right, one at Elwha; below left, one at Port Gamble.

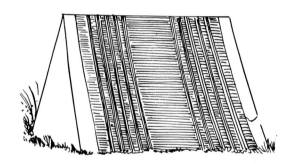

Sketch of burial house with two coffins resting in it was used in Eells' publication *Ten Years of Missionary Work Among the Indians...*

Sketch of burial house was also used by Eells for publication. House was covered with cloth and blanket.

The custom of not speaking aloud the Indian name of the deceased, as Eells explained it, was that

> it makes them feel very badly to be thus reminded of their dead, as if a needle were put into their hearts. It was however once said that the reason was that when the name was pronounced, the dead person turned over in the grave, and Old [Chief] Seattle or his relations, objected very seriously to having that city called by his name, for fear that it would be pronounced very often, and so he would be continually turning, and never have any rest.

Without explaining the reasons for the belief, Eells noted that sepulchures represented five different ages which had "to some extent, coexisted." Of those in the ground:

> There are places where skeletons and parts of them have been plowed up or still remain in the ground, and near together in such a way as to give ground for the belief that formerly Indians were buried in the ground and not in regular cemeteries. Such deposits exist at Doswailopsh, and Hoodsport, among the Twanas, and at Dunginess and Port Angeles, among the Klallams. These graves were made so long ago that the Indians of the present day profess to have no knowledge of the occupants, but believe them to have been their ancestors.

Of canoe burials:

> The most common method as far as the earliest whites have observed, was to bury in canoes. The body was wrapped in mats, blankets or cloth, and placed in a large canoe. Sometimes it was first placed in a box, and then in a canoe, over which a smaller canoe was placed, upside down, to protect the corpse. The canoe was then elevated, perhaps into the forks of two trees, or else on a frame built for the purpose, and left for a year or more. After this sometimes the body was taken down and buried in the ground, but this latter custom, I am satisfied was not universal ... Often the body was elevated near where the death occurred... An old resident has informed me that Clallams always buried their dead in a sitting posture, and I am satisfied that the Twanas often bent theirs up, so that the knees nearly touched the chin...

Eells once saw the doubled-up, emaciated body of an Indian woman which was buried, October, 1877 in a Hudson's Bay Company burial box about 3½ feet long, 1¾ wide, and 1½ high. The day following his own Christian service for her he was invited to her native burial ceremony in which her remains in a box were placed in a canoe and elevated on a scaffold.

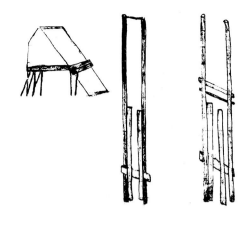

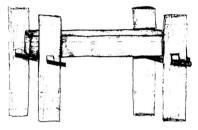

Above left, an infant burial, elevated and covered with cloth. Above right, a part of the scaffolding of an "areial burial" remain. Below, an elevated burial in place.

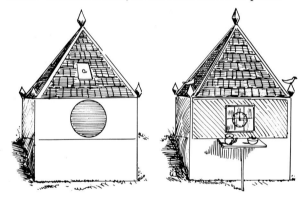

Illustrations are Klallam house burials at Port Gamble which Eells used in his book *Ten Years of Missionary Work Among the Indians.* In front of house on left are several articles left on a shelf. These articles were to be for the use of the deceased.

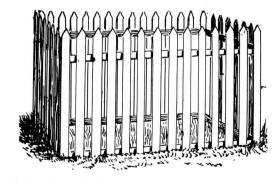

A picket fence built around a burial in the ground.

Of scaffold burials:

About forty years ago, gold mines were discovered on Fraser river in British Columbia, and boats being scarce in this region, unprincipled white men stole many of the canoes in which the dead had been placed and emptied them of their contents. This incensed the Indians, and also caused a change in their mode of burial. They collected their dead in cemeteries, and because enough trees could not be obtained in such places which were suitable for canoes, they built scaffolds for them; but instead of using canoes generally, they made boxes, and elevated them on a frame, and when they did use canoes, they cut holes in them so as to render them useless for any other purpose.

Ruins of one such graveyard were some two miles from the Skokomish Reservation when Eells first went there, although the dead had been moved previously.

"Sometimes," explained Eells, "the boxes were placed near the ground, and articles were hung on posts and upper cross pieces. Sometimes the coffin boxes were elevated a few feet. Several such burials have taken place since I came here, but all were afterwards put under ground." He described another way of placing coffins taken from scaffold, enclosing them in small houses. In one house, "six coffins were placed...one after another, it having been a kind of family vault. Some were laid on the ground, and others immediately on them. They were there in 1874, and I know not how long previously. In 1878, they were put under ground." "Another Twana grave house of different shape," he went on, "had in it two coffins, one resting on the ground, and the other on it, barely covered with earth. Around such graves, clothes, flags and similar articles were placed often on poles." Continuing his explanation of such burials:

Sometimes these grave enclosures were in the shape of a small house, sometimes merely like the roof of a house; sometimes they were covered or partially covered with cloth or blankets, and sometimes they had nothing of the kind on the boards of which they were made. Sometimes no articles were placed near them, but often lying near by on the ground or perhaps on a shelf, built for the purpose were dishes, lamps, tin pails, a tub, beads, clothes, canoes, and similar articles, generally broken so as to be useless to thieves, but not always so. Some are surrounded by a good paling fence, and some are not. I once saw dishes containing water at Port Gamble in which were floating small American rubber toys. Sometimes these houses are painted, but generally they are not. Sometimes the coffin rests on the ground, sometimes it is raised a little and sometimes the house is made so closely that I could not see how the coffin was placed.

Eells discovered that as the Indians came more in contact with whites, they learned to bury in the ground. In preparation for such burials, they usually obtained

a cheap coffin, of American style, put the body in it, and with it a number of articles, chiefly cloth, or clothes, and keepsake articles, which the deceased valued highly, and occasionally money. I have heard of a Clallam chief who was buried with a twenty dollar piece in each hand, and another in his mouth. As a rule, however, money is too valuable for them to use much of it for this purpose, and, besides, the temptation is too great for some one to rob the grave, as unprincipled white men have occasionally done. An Indian I think has never been known to do such a thing, partly from superstitious fear I presume. The body, when I have seen it put in the coffin, is generally wrapped and tied hand and foot and face, and head; cloth, either white cotton or calico is laid in the coffin, and the body put in on the cloth, in such a way that the cloth comes around the sides, and encloses the body; more is put over, partly folded and partly jammed in until the coffin is full. I have also often seen other things, usually the old clothes of the deceased, thrown into the grave and buried. Sometimes I have seen them carried off into the woods and left, a few rods from the grave. Sometimes a house, similar to those already described is built over the grave, and sometimes only a picket fence, and at times the grave is left entirely unprotected. Occasionally where there is no protection, several poles are erected on which cloth and various articles are hung.

In later years, Twanas, Puyallups, Upper Chehalis, Port Madison, Snohomish, most of the Klallams, and other groups had adopted the American custom of placing no gifts or articles of any kind around graves, and of building paling fences around graves or good fences around cemeteries. Eells called these, "civilized burials." Making them more so in his thinking were grave stones and expensive monuments which were sometimes used, especially among the Puyallups whom he thought more "advanced" in this respect. But in 1878, when the Twanas began a new cemetery in the white manner, many of them clung to the custom of placing articles on the coffins.

In fact, wrote Eells, "Those attending a funeral are expected to bring some present to be placed in the coffin, or around the grave... [,] pieces of cloth by women." For several years after Eells came, very few presents had been distributed at graves, but after a time the custom was revived among Twanas, even when burying in "civilized style." Presents usually consisted of half a dollar or a dollar to each man present and half a dollar and perhaps some calico to each woman. Two reasons were given for the practice according to Eells: "One is that these articles are a remembrance of the deceased ... that they are to pay the friends for attending the funeral, for if they should not do so, hardly anyone would attend..." The other reason "was that they believed that as the articles decayed, they were taken by the attending spirits to the abode of the dead, particle by particle, and there put together again, for the use of the deceased. They also believed that the body was carried to the same place in a similar manner."

Old cemeteries which Eells had seen were near the beach, not far from dwellings, and fronting the water, arranged "very irregularly," probably, he thought, for convenience sake as with only canoes to carry their dead it was not easy to take them far back from the shore. Later, with wagons, it was possible to transport bodies some distance from the water, at least among Twanas, Klallams and Puyallups.

Of the common practice of removing the dead, the missionary wrote:

When they [the Indians] arrived at the cemetery the medicine man tore down an inclosure where two of his children had been buried with four other children, relations. Another medicine man, belonging to the same clan, also tore down an inclosure where the bodies of two of his children were placed along with those of two others, their relations. Two of these corpses were above ground and two below. The coffins beneath the ground could not be taken up, but the clothes around the bodies were so well preserved there was no difficulty in removing them. One of the coffins made for one of the children just deceased, was large enough to contain two bodies, so another body, long previously deceased, was put with it. Other rude boxes were made of such capacity as to admit of twelve children being put into eight of the boxes and coffins, most of the old coffins being broken open, and the bodies taken out...The corpse originally in [one] coffin, was lying with its knees near its chin, but all were not so, as some had been laid out straight...A large grave was dug near by, about

12 feet long and 5 wide and 4 deep, lined with mats, and all the boxes and coffins were placed in it, completely covering the bottom of the grave. Several of these boxes were wrapped with many thicknesses of calico; while quilts, blankets, shawls, calico, and a few fancy articles of beadwork and a few small boxes were placed in the coffins with the bodies. All the coffins were next covered with several layers of calico, blankets, mats, and cedar boards to the depth of about 8 inches. An old man then made some remarks, followed by a speech from the child's father, and when this was concluded the grave was filled with earth, a little new calico having been thrown in with the dirt. Next all gathered on the beach, a fire was built on which two or three pieces of cloth were burned, a few men made presents to the fathers of the children just deceased, some calico was given by the women to the mothers, and the two fathers, with another medicine man, presented small sums of money to all the men present, each one giving at least one dollar to every man ... [Women relatives of the deceased] gave about five yards of calico to every woman present. As the old boxes and coffins were opened, the bodies were often handled quite roughly. Only a few persons handled them, and they were chiefly medicine men.

Eells thought that formerly they had been very "superstitious" about going near the dead, making it difficult for him to induce them to attend Christian funeral services. "As they have become more civilized," he concluded, "I have noticed some singular changes in these superstitions."

Suggested Reading

Yarrow, H. A. "A Further Contribution to the Study of the Mortuary Customs of the North American Indians," *First Annual Report of the Bureau of Ethnology to the Secretary of the Smithsonian Institution 1879-'80,* Washington, 1881.
Meany, Edmond S. *Vancouver's Discovery of Puget Sound,* Portland, 1957.

12: RELIGION

Perhaps because he was a clergyman, Eells was extremely interested in native religions, devoting five chapters of his notes to them in contrast to the various other aspects of Indian life to which he devoted no more than single chapters. In this and the ensuing one, "Religion, Tamanous or Sacred Rites," he recorded with reasonable objectivity many of the natives' beliefs and practices as well as the material elements accompanying them.

He best described native religions as those in which

> The practical part...is a compound of shamanism and spiritualism, called in the Chinook Jargon to-máh-no-ûs, a word which has been locally adopted into English, as it is very expressive, meaning a combination of ideas, for which we have no equivalent in English, except by the use of one or more sentences. It is derived from a word in the old Chinook language, it-a-mah-na-was. In general it means anything supernatural either among good or bad spirits, between the Supreme Being on one side, and Satan on the other. Hence both good and bad Tamahnous are spoken of. The word is used as a noun, adjective and verb. As a noun, Tamahnous is the spirit or supernatural being in the other world, which has an influence over man, as his guardian spirit, or the spirit which makes him sick or kills him; also the act of invoking the good ones, and driving away the bad ones, so that a great tamahnous is often spoken of, meaning a great gathering of people, who are performing their incantations. As an adjective, it qualifies and defines certain persons and things, so that a tamahnous man is one, who by his incantations, can influence the spirits,—a medicine man; a tamahnous stick or stone, or painting is one, in which the spirits are believed to dwell; or which is sometimes used in performing their incantations. It is likewise a verb, and to tamanous is to perform the incantations necessary to influence these spirits. In some cases it is done mainly by the medicine men, but in others by any one.

Under a section entitled "Objects of Reverence and Worship," he wrote that these consisted of "the Supreme Being, Dokibatl, angelic spirits, Satan and demons, tamahnous sticks, stones, drawings ... idols and the sun." He believed the concept of Dokibatl but dimly formed and of not much practical value to the natives. It was Dokibatl, he wrote, "who came to the earth, long after the creation of the world, and some say that the world was created by him, long before he came to the world, while others think that it was

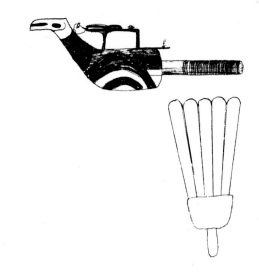

Above, a Haida rattle, imported by Klallams and used in a black tamanous ceremony in Dungeness in 1878. Below to right, is the outline of a rattle which Eells was permitted to look at long enough to sketch an outline but not the full detail of thunderbird face on it. It was quadrilateral in shape with fan tail.

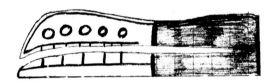

A bird mask with a "mouth" that opened and shut with a hinge. Eells found this one on a Klallam grave.

Black tamanous rattle made by carving and hollowing out two pieces of wood, filling the instrument with pebbles and tieing together with strings and wrapping the handle. Back was painted black; underside, red. It was shaken in circular movement.

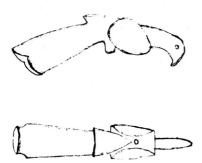

Front and side view of tamanous powder charge, thought to assist hunters to have good kills.

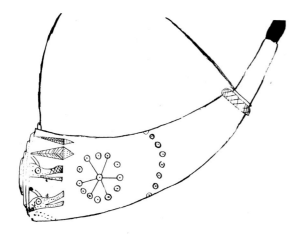

Black Tamanous powder horn decorated with wolf heads.

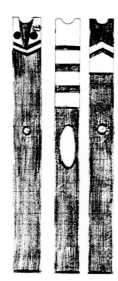

Tamanous posts which supported the ridge pole of an old potlatch house at Port Angeles. These painted posts reached from the ground to the cone of the roof.

created by a Supreme Being other than him. If the ideas of the latter class were held before the coming of the whites, then they had a dim idea of a Great Spirit. I am also told that they had a dim idea of a great being who created the sun, long before they knew of Dokibatl, but that they never speak his name." An old Klallam man informed the missionary that before the coming of whites they knew nothing of God, but worshipped the sun as their God to which they daily prayed, saying "'Sun, take care of me,' and they gave food to it at noon." The natives, wrote Eells, also believed that the first whites which came to the Sound in their vessel were Dokibatl.

As to the genesis of men, an Indian told Eells a story which the missionary thought quite similar to that found in the Bible, causing him to believe it to have been based on a mixture of biblical teachings of whites and old myths. According to the account, Dokibatl

> made man out of the ground, and a woman out of his rib, and gave them a good land, telling them to eat all the fruit, except one kind of berries; but the woman, tempted by Skwai-il, the king of evil, ate of those berries. When Dokibatl came, he said, 'Have you been eating of those berries?' She said, 'No.' He replied, 'Yes, I know you have.' On account of this her children became Indians, ignorant, foolish, and dark skinned. The man however did not eat of the berries, and to his children were given letters, the knowledge of books, and a white skin.

The natives also had a tradition of a deluge. After that, according to their tradition

> The Great Spirit, seeing their deplorable condition, and taking pity on them, sent over the mountains from the east, a tamahnous man, or savior, whose countenance was as the sun, and voice as the thunder, and he was armed with a bow, arrows and spear...He then taught them of the existence of two great spirits,—one of good and one of evil ... [H]e again called the people together, and held a big potlatch, giving to the Indians, what appeared to them, at the time, great curiosities.

These curiosities were bows and arrows, canoes, fish hooks, camas sticks, baskets and fire, all of which he taught them how to use.

Of "Angelic spirits": "Every man and nearly every woman formerly was thought to have one which was called his or her tamanous. Such a spirit was supposed to guard the man or woman who often communed with it in the dark, when alone in the woods, and, by various incantations, invoked its aid in time of need. These angels were the most useful deities they had, and the practice of invoking their aid was the most practical part of their religion." One Indian told Eells they did not worship a multitude of spirits, but only asked them to intercede before the deity for the people. Eells thought it not improbable, that the practice was derived from the Roman Catholic faith of praying to saints as taught them by a priest of that faith among them forty years earlier.

Just as there were benevolent spirits there were also malignant ones whose favor, Eells believed, the natives devoted much of their tamanous to conquer or to gain its aid and favor. He believed their idea of sickness was founded on this belief in malignant spirits which medicine men sought to counteract. "They believe," wrote Eells, "that these spirits, both good and bad, may dwell at times in certain sticks or stones, hence these ... become objects of reverence or fear. The sticks are generally reverenced at all times, for, although the spirit dwells there only a small portion of the time, yet after it has been given to the spirit by its earthly owner that spirit is supposed to always watch over it and be angry with any one who treats it disrespectfully."

Some of these spirits, according to native belief, supported potlatch houses in the form of cedar posts. They were from one and a half to two and a half feet wide, and from eight to ten feet long, sometimes painted and figured. Eells thought the Indians very careless about protecting them, although "quite superstitious about allowing any one to desecrate them, for fear that the spirits ... would become angry..." Then, recounting some of his own experiences with these posts:

> Several years after they were made and placed in position, in 1881, a heavy snow crushed the house, and the posts were scattered around promiscuously in the ruins. A few of their owners removed theirs to their dwellings, but others did not take care of them, but allowed them to be knocked around, until they were knocked into the water of Hood Canal and floated away. They seemingly acted on the principle, that while it was wrong for a person to abuse them, yet when the elements abused them, the spirits must take care of them, or they would not be cared for. After some years however, they lost their fear of them, and I was allowed to take a few of the poorer ones, which remained, though at that time, the paint had all been washed off...The cross beams on which these which support the ridge pole, in the potlatch houses, rest, are also believed to be sacred, although they are neither carved or painted...If any person knocks one of these down so that it falls on the ground, it is said to make the spirit which dwells in them so angry that he may send sickness upon the whole tribe.

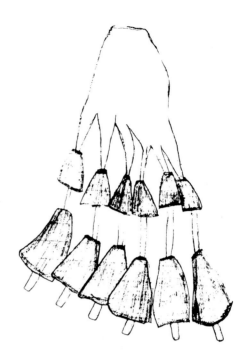

Deer-hoof rattles held in hands or fastened to waist in some forms of tamanousing.

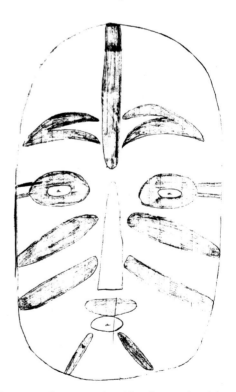

Klallam mask painted with charcoal with nose of separate piece of wood.

Klallam mask used in black tamahnous. Painted with various colors, it had nostril openings through which persons wearing it could see out.

Two years after Eells had collected a crossbeam from a long deserted communal house there was considerable sickness among the Indians and some deaths among the children. One Indian hinted to him that it was he, the missionary, that had caused the sickness by angering a spirit. Eventually, as Eells observed, the Indians had little apprehension about such things, permitting him to obtain some of the sacred beams which he sketched.

Eells further explained that these tamanous representations were on the door of an owner's house, sometimes at the head of a bed and sometimes even on a powder charge, the idea being that the tamanous would guard the house and its occupants, protecting its owner when asleep and helping him when hunting.

Another kind of tamanous stick was about seven to ten feet long, round, two or three inches in diameter at each end and about an inch thicker in the middle. It was painted very simply, black on one side, and red on the other. Originally, when this stick was very valuable, natives would give a horse to someone for making them a pair of them.

The missionary had been in the country but a short time before becoming satisfied that "the principle of idolatry was here." "I had," he con-

tinued, "been here four years before I saw what could be called by this name ... in 1878 I saw it...about four feet long, roughly carved, with the face and body of a man, but with no legs or feet, the lower part being set into the ground, and around this they performed their incantations [to "tamanous" for lost spirits]." Twanas had told him that Klallams at Port Discovery had large idols ten or twelve feet long which they had worshipped long before. Kept in the woods, these had by Eells' time nearly decayed. Two somewhat similar images had also been found in the woods up the Skokomish River.

Tamanous sticks used in connection with the images were held in the hand during ceremonies and were believed to have contained spirits. Some of these

were about four feet long ... painted red, one had in addition a little blue paint, and some were not painted. A band of cedar bark was wound around each one not far from a foot from the upper end in a place cut for it. They were sharpened at the lower end, and when not in actual use, were stuck in the ground around the image. One of them was carved in such a way that it seemed as if the first part, a foot long, entered, wedge like, into the rest, and this was said to represent a shark's tongue ... These unlike the idol had been recently made, for the occasion; and each one was owned by a single individual, though I thought that sometimes the same one was used by others than the owner ... When not in use their head bands were hung on them. I once saw a broken one...and these are all I have seen during the twenty years I have been here. I supposing they kept them concealed in the woods.

Eells once asked an Indian to make hand sticks for him, but the red man declined, saying that if he did, the rest of the Indians would be angry with him. Although the sticks were not intended for "profane hands" the Indians readily granted Eells the privilege of making drawings of them.

Eells explained that during ceremonies as those in which hands sticks were used, as well as in many other forms of the tamanous, headbands, usually of beaten cedar bark about an inch in diameter with one or more feathers in them, were also used: "In black tamahnous these bands are generally colored black, and the ends of the feathers are tipped black, but in other kinds of tamahnous they remain their natural color." Another implement he noted as being used in the ceremonies, was the drum: Those used by the Twanas and most of the upper Sound Indians

have a square or rectangular head, the sides of which are from a foot to two or more feet in length.

They are made of skin, usually deer skin, stretched over a wooden frame. Each drum has only one head. On the reverse side two leather thongs or straps are crossed at right angles, to form a handle ... The Clallams usually make their drums with a round head, but similar in all other respects to the Twana drum...I have a Twana one—which was used by a medicine man, when doctoring a sick child. The child died and the drum was broken through the head and thrown away as no good. These drums are used on nearly all religious occasions, in black and red tamahnous, in doctoring the sick, and gambling, in fact, whenever the help of the spirits is invoked.

Then, of another implement, the rattle:

One variety is made of deer hoofs ... strung in quite large bunches. I have also seen blank rifle shells mixed with them. These rattles are held in the hands or fastened to the waist or other parts of the body, while tamahnousing. I do not know that they are ever used in tamahnous for the sick, or in the black tamahnous ... The Clallams also have rattles made of the scallop shells, which are found in their waters...A hole is made near the hinge of each shell, and a number of them are strung on a small stick about the size of a lead pencil ... which is bent in a circular form and serves for a handle. These are shaken edgewise, so that the edge cuts through the air. If they should be shaken sideways, they are liable to be broken, by striking against each other, and if they should be thus broken, the person holding them would die shortly ... The black tamahnous rattle is somewhat in the shape of a bird, but hollow, and is used in the black tamahnous ceremonies ... shaken with a kind of circular movement, being held in one hand. They are considered very sacred.

Sometimes painted black with red, green and yellow, or with no color at all, these "tyee" (chief) rattles were of various shapes. They "were used at great festivals to call the people together early in the morning." Others were "constructed on the same principle, that is hollow, and with stones inside ... occasionally imported from the Haida and Clyoquote [Clayoquot] of British Columbia, who are expert carvers. These are painted various colors, and though not black were used in the black tamahnous ceremonies."

Eells noted three mask styles also used in the ceremonials: those representing the human face in honor of the performer, a man; those representing a bird, in honor of the thunderbird; and those representing the wolf, in honor of that animal which had taught man the mysteries of the thunderbird performance. Although he had never seen masks used by Twanas, such face coverings were used in his time by Klallams in their black

tamanous ceremonies. He described them as often "made in the shape of a man's face, with more or less blue, red, and black paint on them, much as they would paint their faces at times ... Others are made in the shape of the head of a bird or wolf... Another kind opens like a bird's mouth, and shuts again, with a hinge, operated by a string." Other implements used in the tamanous were furnished Eells by a Skokomish Reservation woman. These were

from three to seven inches long, a quarter to half an inch in diameter, at the upper end, and are made of human hair, gathered in small bunches, and wound at one end, so as to fasten the hair together. They are wound with strings, ribbons, and strings of beads. Some have pink and red feathers with the hair. A few have small pieces of iron, an inch or two long, in the upper end, covered with ribbon, tape or beads.

Sharpened sticks seven or eight inches long and three-quarters of an inch in diameter with cloth often tied around the upper ends for handles were also used in the black tamanous ceremonies by participants striking them wildly as they ran.

Of special interest to Eells, the missionary, was what he called their "Ecclesiastical organization." He found it had no special classes or persons as priests, and, that there was much individualism in their tamanous worship. He noted that medicine men, "because of the power they are supposed to have with spirits," were greatly feared, charging large fees, sometimes in advance, not only for curing the sick but making persons sick at the request of their enemies. He noted hazards in the profession as when they failed to effect cures. Formerly they were occasionally shot for such failures, but after the treaty was made [at Point No Point, January 26, 1855] the Indian agent prohibited death as a punishment. But then, some Indians complained bitterly because as the doctors were allowed to kill people with their tamanous, the people were not allowed to retaliate in kind, their only defense against the doctors.

In 1880, Eells found four women doctors among the Klallams and one of their sex performing among the Squaxins. This reminded him all the more that he lived among a people of the spirit, regardless of sex — or of age — from youthful recipients of guardian spirits to the elderly on the brink of the grave.

As other white men among natives, he found the potlatch of gift-giving, which took its name from the Chinook jargon word, meaning "to give," a peculiar custom in which "the giving of one makes the giver a great man among the other

Old style door was circular aperture cut through a building. Myron Eells saw only one, that in a Klallam house at Sequim. It was 3½ by 3¾ feet, closed by sliding other boards over the aperture.

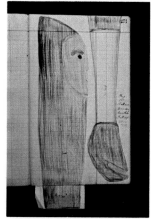

This particular carved and painted wooden war club was made by a Klallam at Dungeness for a "show" when doing their war dances for whites. As Eells noted, this war club was employed in a money making activity. The missionary obtained it in 1894.

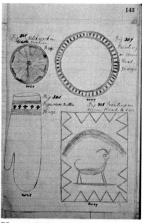

Upper left, patchwork design sewed on pin cushion.
Lower left, figures knitted on mittens.
Upper right, design painted on Klallam drum. Few natives painted their drums.
Lower right, figures painted on drum.

Figures woven in at each end of rug are of a dog.

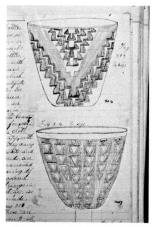

Water-tight baskets with geometric designs made by a Twana.

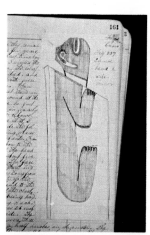

Chinook canoe bows were carved. This one belonged to a Haida.

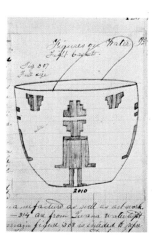

This water-tight basket is designed with figures.

One side of beaded shot pouch of Klallam make.

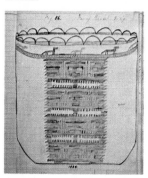

Another representation of skill of Puget Sound Indians was their use of small grasses tightly woven into baskets. By Eells' time aniline dyes to color grasses for ornamentation had replaced native dyes.

Beaded shot pouch imported from British Columbia by Klallams was not beaded on reverse side.

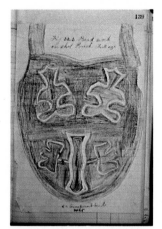

This is the reverse side of the beaded cloth shot pouch as illustrated on the preceeding page.

Water-tight baskets made by Twanas.

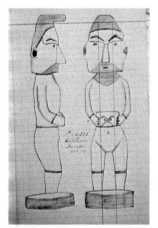

Carving of man by a Klallam. The man, ready for potlatching, was dressed in few clothes. He held carving of face in his hands.

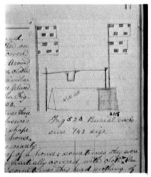

Burial with a number of flags.

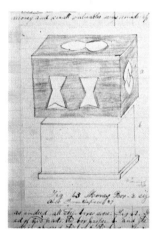

Money give-aways had always been a part of potlatching. Old style money was dentalium shells stored in money boxes made in two parts — the box proper and the cover enclosing all sides to the bottom. Sides of each were made with one board kerfed for corners, steamed and pegged in place, one to a bottom piece, the other to a top.

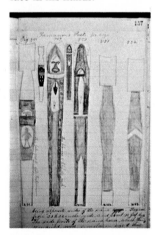

Tamanous posts from house built on Skokomish Reservation in 1875-76. These posts supported the ridgepole of a potlatch house. Two on the left were owned separately by different individuals.

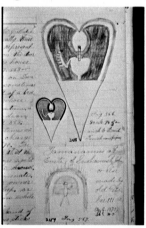

Each person had a tamanous spirit to protect him in times of illness as well as danger. Each believed that spirits lived in tamanous boards. Above is one carved in shape of heart, 24 inches wide and 56 inches long, and painted red, white, and blue. Attached in space in upper part of heart was glass pitcher handle. The board was nailed to sidepost of a potlatch house on the Squaxin Reservation.

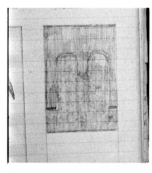

To destroy a tamanous board was believed to have made one ill. Any board, such as the door to a dwelling, a canoe paddle, or as above, a head board from a bed was used on which to paint a tamanous.

Indians." Activities included dancing, gambling, feasting and tamanousing in addition to the potlatch proper.

A changing economy produced changes in the potlatch giveaways. In the later years of his ministry, Eells realized that several persons combined to give potlatches because of their increased expense: "They have grown so large, however, that seldom does even the richest person feel able alone to give one, hence they combine together, sometimes twenty or thirty being concerned in the same one." Yet, the old vestiges remained— erecting of special houses for them, sending of invitations to guests, the elaborate landing ceremonies on the arrival of guests:

> In the distribution, all the invited ones do not receive equal amounts, but special friends, the young and strong, and those who expect soon to make a potlatch, generally receive the most, in order that their favor may be gained, so that when they shall make one, they will be liberal to those making the present one, but the old, and those not expected to make one do not receive very much, as, according to their ideas, it would be a poor investment to give to such persons. Sometimes, indeed, instead of calling it a gift, they call it a paying back for money once received. This has been especially the case when they have been urged to cease the practice; they have replied, that as they have received money at such times, it would be much like stealing it were they not to make a potlatch and return it.

Eells kept a list of potlatches to which some of the Twanas and Klallams had been invited, but later abandoned his practice because "the Indians had become so civilized that the potlatches became less frequent." Not since about 1880 was he aware that any of the various peoples around him, with one exception, had given a potlatch. During the period from 1874 to 1879, by contrast, they had been held more frequently. During the period of time they were held he did note changes in the kinds of goods given away. These represented a mixture of native and American products—fancy cedar bark mats, various types of baskets, large spoons, long beads and salmon, bolts of calicoes, blankets, horses, beeves, guns and silver and gold coins. He also noted that times for holding potlatches had changed: "Of late years the celebration of this day [July the Fourth] has largely taken the place of the potlatch. In doing this, they usually differ from the white man's celebration. They spend nearly a week at it, feasting, visiting, horse racing, and the like. One man is at the head of it, and bears the brunt of the expense, assisted

Wood carving of human face made for amusement, with apparently no other function. Open spaces at each "x".

however by some others. There is at times a distribution of gifts, though not always."

He thought the demise of potlatches near:

> At present their glory is departing in this region. Many of the younger people, who have been in contact with the whites for the past twenty-five years, have become ashamed to go through many of the practices, which were formerly the most savage and the most interesting; they have invented nothing new to take their places, so that the last one which I attended was called very dry by the chief. They are likewise slowly learning that their money can be of more use to them in some other way than to give it away. Probably to the north, where their civilization is less rapid, they will last sometime longer.

Suggested Reading

Colson, Elizabeth. *The Makah Indians,* Manchester, England, 1953.

Bancroft, Hubert Howe. *The Works of Hubert Howe Bancroft,* I, San Francisco, 1883.

Swan, James G. *The Northwest Coast,* New York, 1857.

13: RELIGION, TAMANOUS OR SACRED RITES

"In general," wrote Eells, "tamahnous may be divided into three parts, the red tamahnous, black tamahnous, and tamahnous for the sick. In the first, the people paint their faces red, in the second, black, and in the third the rites are controlled by the medicine men, with usually no paint." He found the red tamanous to have been a common form of worship in which the natives' objective was to gain from their tamanous what they wished "as the Christian prays for various things" or "the same principle that a Christian or Mohamadan prays to his God—that is to obtain help and protection, and success." Thus, the aid could be invoked for wind when traveling in canoes or in gambling games played with round disks.

Eells called another type, "crazy tamahnous," which he admitted he did not fully understand, but was satisfied the "crazy feeling" was caused by the effect of the imagination: "It is said that a bad tamahnous attacks a person, who becomes crazy, and then there must be a regular work of tamahnous, so as to drive out the bad spirit."

Of the tamanous quest:

The first thing for a young man to do by way of sacred rites was to find his tamahnous. In order to do this I am told that a father would send his son into the woods or mountains, a long ways from home, where he was not allowed to eat for a period of from ten to thirteen days, though he was required to bathe often, and keep up a good fire. They say that such fasting would kill a man, under ordinary circumstances, but that his tamahnous keeps him alive, though he has not yet seen or found it. At last his tamahnous reveals itself to him in the shape, ordinarily of a bird or beast, which afterwards is sacred to him. The women also have their tamahnous, which they find in much the same way.

A white man, who had a Twana wife, and who formerly lived near Eells, told the missionary that from his observation he was satisfied that when a bad tamanous got hold of a person, he could not eat, or if he did, was compelled to vomit up the food. He said he had often seen his wife in that condition, but was satisfied that she feigned nothing, but it was the "bad tamanous" causing the trouble. At such times, he said, she acted in a crazy manner, and it was useless for her to try to eat, until her friends tamanoused with her, and

drove away the evil spirit after which she recovered her usual health. Of these statements, Eells believed there was nothing "which cannot...be explained by the laws of the imagination, but the Indian has never studied mental philosophy, and so knows nothing of those laws, but attributed all to tamahnous."

He thought what he termed "Tamahnous for the living" to have been somewhat allied to the "crazy tamahnous," in that the candidate selected the time and place to be sick, sometimes laying plans for it a year or two in advance and even building a house for it which was later torn down or used as a barn or shed. Because it usually occurred in the winter, "when there is little else to do," it was sometimes called "winter tamahnous."

Of another tamanous type which Eells termed "Propitiatory tamahnous," he wrote:

It has often been more difficult for me to learn the principles and reasons of a tamahnous, than to get an opportunity to observe the ceremonies, but I have reason to believe that this one was performed in order to cleanse their hearts from the evil which they had done, which would offend their tamahnous. Such ceremonies have been very common during the long winter nights."

Of another type which he termed "The Spirit Land tamahnous or tamahnous for lost spirits," he wrote that the Indians believed that in the spirit land, people lived and died, just as in this world, and when they died in that land, they came back into the world where they were born again and lived:

Sometimes the people of the spirit land come up into this world, and get the spirits of their relatives, so that they may soon die, and so the sooner join them. After this the person whose spirit has been taken wastes away or dies suddenly. If by any means it is discovered that this has been done...then they attempt to get the spirit back by a tamanous and if it is done the person will live. Sometimes a person who is believed to have intercourse with the other world persuades one who is in the best of health that he has visited the spirit land and seen the spirit of his dupe there, and the latter is thus frightened into having a tamanous. Again, when some credulous individual has been ailing a little or a long time, but not sufficiently to feel that he needs to employ a medicine man, one of these arrant humbugs takes a fancied journey to the land of shades to search for the lost soul of the invalid ... Frequently in the winter when time hangs heavily on their hands and they are at a loss for amusements these soul searchers pretend that they have received tidings of a number of errant spirits and they get up a general spirit hunt ... carried on mostly in the night...The breaking of the ground is an important part of the ceremony. The surface of the earth is often actually broken in order, they say, that the spirits of those who are performing can descend into the other world. When, as they pretend, the descent is accomplished, they represent pantomimically that they travel along a road, cross at least one stream, and travel on until they come to a place where the spirits dwell. Men only act the part of travelers in the nether world, though women and children are present at the tamahnous. When they are supposed to cross the stream, they actually set up some boards on opposite sides of a beam in the house, which was about ten feet from the ground...to represent the bridge. They crawled up the board on one side, and down on the other. If in going down a man should slip, they believe he will die within a year.

He wrote that but eight men went through this journey in 1878, but nearly all the other people were present pounding sticks and singing their tamanous songs to the accompaniment of a drum. Having discovered that underground spirits had possession of those spirits of this world, the travelers surprised and fought them:

On one evening [the returning travelers] professed to recover and bring back to this world the spirits of three persons which they pretended to roll up in cloth...and work over for some time, after which they seemed to give them to their real owners ... While performing these ceremonies, they used the hand sticks ... wore the head band, and danced around the idol."

The missionary described the black tamanous as "a secret religious society," whose rites were by far the most "savage" to him of any practiced by the Indians. When going through the ceremonies "they always painted their faces more or less black...The strips are about the width of a finger. I have however seen them painted all conceivable patterns, spot, spots, stripe, stripes, a part, or the whole of the face wholly black." The strenuous ceremony was performed in honor of the mythical thunderbird, originating, Eells was told, after two men quarreled over a woman. Over barnacles, one of them dragged the bleeding body of the other who all the time feigned death. Then, when about to be eaten by wolves, he jumped up and escaped, such brave action so pleasing to the "Chief Wolf" that he taught the man the mysteries of the thunderbird performance. Eells found this ceremony held among natives from Puget Sound northward.

Eells made this refined drawing, one he did from a sketch made for him by an Indian to show a "tamahnous sick," no. 2. No. 1 shows the way the sick proceeded to kill a person; no. 3 is a second "tamahnous sick" which hung over Indian artist's brother; no. 4 was not identified; no. 5 is another sickness.

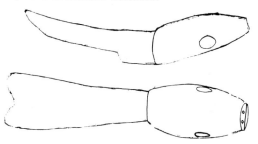

Eells believed this carved piece found on the Skokomish Reservation to have been a tamahnous hand stick. It was 8 inches long.

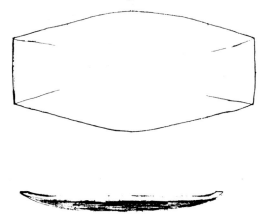

At religious feasts food was often served on large, shallow, wooden troughs, usually of alderwood. Short troughs were used for family eating.

In it

The performers hoot like owls, howl like wolves, paint their bodies black, especially the face ... scarify their arms, legs, and sometimes the body, so as to bleed profusely, in remembrance of its origin; they make much noise, by firing guns, pound on drums to represent thunder, flash torches of pitchwood about as a representation of lightning, and whistle sharply in imitation of wind. The ceremonies, however, vary in different tribes, being much more savage and bloody in some than in others. Among the Makah five days are usually occupied in secret ceremonies, such as initiating candidates and other performances, before any public outdoor ceremonies take place. Among the Clallam the candidate for initiation is put into a kind of mesmeric sleep, which does not appear to be the case with the Makahs. Among the Clallam, however, the secret ceremonies are not always as long as among the Makahs, as the only time the writer ever witnessed the public exercises he was admitted very soon after they began, though there were secret ceremonies during the whole five days of the performance, in a house or behind a blanket. The affair closes with a general distribution of presents to the invited guests.

An early white resident of the area, who had witnessed the ceremonies around the mid-"sixties," told Eells that a candidate for initiation into the society was starved for a long time and closely watched. Someone else told Eells that formerly candidates were so starved that they tore living dogs to pieces with their teeth. There was also cutting of the body and limbs quite deeply so that these candidates became bloody, without taking note of it. The missionary had never heard of cannibalism among the Sound Indians, but believed it would not have been strange because Tsimshian Indians of British Columbia often tore dogs to pieces and chewed pieces out of living persons in some of their "savage orgies," and Makahs made great noises firing off guns to imitate thunder, and gashed their arms, legs and bodies, "five or six inches long, and from an eighth to a quarter of an inch deep."

He described tamanousing at a February, 1878 Twana potlatch held the day after church services. On the day of the services the Indians had been "too much excited to give up the whole day to rest, tamahnousing instead." During the evening of their own native ceremony, Sooke Indians of lower Vancouver Island jumped around and made violent movements.

Eells thought "Tamahnous over the sick" more powerful over the Indian mind than any other, being more germane to their lives than any of the others. "Hence the order in which they have abandoned their tamahnous has been first, the black tamahnous, as the most savage, and least reasonable; second, the red tamahnous, which embodied the main part of their religion; and lastly, the tamahnous over the sick, which, while it contained some elements of religion, also contained much superstition." Eells thought the foundation of this kind of tamanous to have been the "medicine men."

"A wicked medicine man can," he wrote,

as they believe, in an invisible manner shoot a stone, ball, or poison into the heart of a person to make him sick. They believe this so firmly that they say when the heart of one who died was opened the stone or bone has been found in it. He is also supposed to be able to send a woodpecker, squirrel, bear, or any treacherous animal to the heart of his enemy to eat his heart, plague him, make him sick, or kill him."

They could perform their work from considerable distances, the missionary remembered, as in one case where a Skokomish Reservation Indian threatened to make some Port Gamble Indians ill. When they became so, they believed the sickness to have been sent by a Twana medicine man hired for the purpose. Indians, other than medicine men, were believed to have had powers to make people ill. As a rule most Twana medicine men did not attend church much, "and when I have asked them, the reason why, I have been told that the other Indians have been afraid to have them go, where they would be in so close contact with them." Some Indians told Eells they were afraid to have medicine men touch them, because these doctors had special poisons they could rub on people to make them ill. He thought this practice uncommon; otherwise, it would have become commonly known, and whites would have learned what the poison was.

He stressed the psychological factors in illnesses:

I am satisfied however, that when a person becomes sick, who perhaps has been threatened, or even who may not have been threatened, even though the sickness may be light, yet that he believes it has been sent into him by a medicine man, and that this effect of the imagination greatly increases the sickness; and so the person can hardly be cured without another medicine man to assist, and this faith in this Indian doctor greatly helps to cure him.

In curing the sick

the good medicine man tries to find out from the sickness, what kind of a tamahnous has been sent into the individual, and in what manner; whether in the shape of an animal, stone, or otherwise, and from where it has been sent; then by means of his incantations he tries to draw it out. In this work he is the leader, but is usually assisted by some of the common people, both men and women, from a half a dozen to twenty or more in number. These take small sticks in their hands, about a foot and a half long, and a half an inch or an inch in diameter, and pound on the floor, or on large sticks or rails in front of them. I have never learned that these sticks are considered sacred. They are split out of any common stick for the occasion, are very rough, and are thrown away, when the persons are done using them. One person beats the drum, and all sing an accompaniment to the noise, at least a chorus. In the meantime the medicine man sings a solo, and places his hands on some part of the body and draws forth, or says he does, the evil spirit, and when he says he has it he holds it between his hands, invisible, and blows it up or takes it to another man who throws a stone at it and kills it, or drowns it in water in a vessel nearby. When the sick person is not cured they say there are several evil spirits, but sometimes the person dies before they are all drawn out or else the opposing medicine man is stronger than he and so he can not draw them all out. Sometimes he says that the good spirit of the invalid, the life sustaining principle is gone, having been taken away, and he tries to find where it has gone, get it, and restore it.

Eells thought that whites treated in the same manner would have died, and, that enough Indians recovered to strengthen their faith in their native practitioners. He thought that in treating diseases like rheumatism these doctors did very little good or harm, but did much harm in treating brain diseases, measles, whooping cough and the like. In the spring of 1878 when measles prevailed among Twana children, their parents followed orders of their agency physician, but when the children began to recover, their elders tamanoused over them apparently, thought Eells, to get the credit for curing them; but their exposure to the weather and applications of cold water being too severe for many of the little ones, they died. He noted that Klallams at Dungeness had undergone a similar experience a few years earlier.

In explaining recovery from illnesses, Eells opined that there may have been some sort of mesmeric power at work wielded by the medicine men affecting the patient favorably, an opinion shared by Dr. B. F. Tolmie, a long-time Hudson's Bay Company physician at Fort Nisqually who had seen the impact of mesmeric powers in demonstrations in London. There was "actual medical practice," for "occasionally the medicine men suck blood from their patients...on the same principle as cupping. I have been able to suck blood from my own arm, and presume that Indian doctors can do the same." But above all, Eells was satisfied that some of the cures were attributable to the confidence which the Indians had in their medicine men: "It is the power of the mind over the body."

In 1883, a Twana woman who, after telling the missionary she had given up all tamanous and had intended living as a Christian, returned to her native doctor after having been given up by the agency physician who thought her lung ailment incurable. She lived for a year and a half after the native doctor's ministrations over her. Wrote Eells of her case: "Fear of a bad tamahnous was quickly killing her, and the removal of that fear, by the tamahnousing of a doctor, relieved her." Of similar victims: "Fear keeps him sick, and only a tamahnous cures him."

Eells told of an Indian, Chehalis Jack, who stood by him and his agent brother in their efforts to "civilize and Christianize" his people, trying to induce them to adopt "civilized" customs. For his efforts, Chehalis Jack was warned that some enemy would send a bad tamanous into him and make him sick. In July, 1881 he became ill with rheumatism and, although attended by the agency doctor, and finding some relief, he eventually grew worse. On returning to a native doctor he exclaimed to Eells, "Tamahnous is true, tamahnous is true. You and your brother have told us it is not, but now I have experienced it, and it keeps me sick." After employing another Indian doctor, he recovered. Again Eells thought it "the effect of the influence of the mind over the body."

The government policy of preventing Indians from ministering to the sick was, stated Eells, "one of the most difficult things the Indian Agent ever tried to do among the Indians." Not until 1885, after several directives from government officials, did the agent believe the time had come to clamp down on the practice. Not long thereafter, a chief's wife became ill, receiving ministrations from a very influential native doctor, Tenas Charley, who was hauled into court for his defiance of the ban against activities of native doctors. Charley continued his defiance, stating that he would never stop his tamanous. Fearful that federal troops would be brought in from Port Townsend, the people pressured Charley to turn himself in. This he did, remaining in jail for ten days and paying a forty-dollar fine. Eells thought it had been good for him since "he learned not to oppose the government."

One time the missionary asked the Indians why their tamanous did not affect white persons, to which they replied that "a white man's heart is hard like a stone, so that the invisible stone which they shoot, cannot affect it, while the Indian's heart is soft, like mud, and thus is easily affected." They also said that a cause of this was "that the Indian swims very much, and often times has his clothes off while at home, and so his heart is susceptible to the influence of the tamahnous, while the white man's customs are different, and so his heart is different."

Eells knew of one or two white men, both illiterate, who had lived with the Indians, and who, when sick, had been tamanoused over by Indian doctors and recovered, thus vowing their faith in the practice.

Eells reported that in the early "eighties" Indians of the Skokomish Reservation had begun losing faith in their old tamanous religion and method of curing the sick. Important in having caused this loss of faith was the fact that

Protestants, Catholics, religious people, and people of no religion, rough loggers with whom they worked and cultivated [cultured] people, all united in one thing, and that was to call their tamahnous very foolish; and in the processes of time it had its effect. The Indians began to lose faith in it. But the Indian is a religious being. He must have some religion. When he gives up one he must have another. When these gave up the tamahnous, a new religion appeared which has been called the Shakes, and its followers the Shakers, from the fact that during their services, their hands, arms and even heads, often shake exceedingly fast. It is evidently an affection of the nerves, and based somewhat on the same principle in human nature as the jerks were, which occurred in the Southwestern states seventy five years ago. It is also akin to the Messiah craze of the Dakota Indians of 1890, having a Messiah in it, but being much more civilized, and with no thought of war. It fairly began in 1882, but there were some preliminaries, which finally connected themselves with it ... [combining] Protestant and Catholic teachings, and the old native superstitions ... [with orientation] largely to heaven.

Suggested Reading

Haeberlin, Hermann and Erna Gunther. *The Indians of Puget Sound, Publications in Anthropology,* IV, 1, University of Washington, Seattle, 1930.

Williams, Johnson. "Black Tamanous, the Secret Society of the Clallam Indians," *Washington Historical Quarterly,* VIII, 4 (October, 1916).

Eells collected drawings made by others, mostly those of school children. This one however, from his notebooks was made prior to 1879 by a talented Klallam boy who had no schooling.

APPENDIX

Eells' Identification and Location of the Tribes

I. *Twanas*—Their name is spelled Too-an-hooch in the treaty which was made in 1855; the Clallams, Squaksons and other Indians pronounce it Tu-an-hu, and the Twanas call it Tu-ad-hu. These various pronounciations have been shortened to Twana, which is now used in all government reports.

They originally lived on both sides of Hood's Canal for its whole length, and were divided into three bands, the Du-hle-lips, Skokomish and Kolsids, or Quil-ceeds.

The Du-hle-lips originally lived at the head of the Canal, where a small stream empties into it, which they called Du-hle-lip, but which the whites now call Union creek, and for about ten miles below the head.

Fifteen miles below the head were the Skokomish band, who lived near the mouth of the Skokomish river, where is the present reservation for the whole tribe. Dr. Gibbs in Vol. I. Contributions to North American Ethnology, gives this as the name of the whole tribe, but it was originally only the name of one band. Now, however, as it is the name of the reservation, the whole tribe is better known to the whites by the name Skokomish than by their original one of Twana.

Thirty or forty miles below the Skokomish river lived the Quilceeds, or Kol-ceedobish as they called themselves, but Kol-sin-o-bish as the Clallams pronounced it. Their home was around the Quilceed Bay, the northernmost arm of Hood's Canal, and the mouth of the Duk-a-boos and Dos-wail-opsh rivers.

These three bands were not always at peace but waged petty wars with each other. For more than thirty years, however, most of them have been gathered on the same reservation, have been on good terms with each other and have intermarried, so that these band distinctions are now practically obsolete. When, however, the older Du-hle-lips leave the reservation, for fishing, they are apt to go to their old waters, and the same is true of the Quilceeds.

The dialects of these three bands formerly varied a little: thus the word for go, in Du-hle-lip, was bi-se-dab, while in Skokomish it was bi-he-dab. But at the present time I have not found it practicable, in collecting a vocabulary, to separate the dialects. I have gathered most of the words from the older school-boys, who have been brought up on the reservation, and who have heard all of the dialects, which are rapidly merging into one. Generally I have found it necessary to use English speaking Indians for the purpose, and the older school-boys are the best there are.

At present most of these Indians live on the Skokomish reservation. About a dozen live around Seabeck and Quil-ceed.

Although the Squakson tribe, by treaty and language, belong to the Nisqually Indians, yet about thirty of that tribe, since the selection of the Skokomish reservation, have moved to it, and have become incorporated with the Twanas. They did so because their own people for a time were scattered, because of the nearness of the reservation to their old haunts and its advantages, and because of numerous intermarriages between them and the Twanas. For the most part, they use their own language, but they understand the Twanas and the Twanas understand them. Twenty-five others for a time became connected with the Twanas, but because they did not obtain titles to the land on the reservation as soon as they expected, and as soon as they had a right to expect from government promises, they became discouraged and left.

II: *The Chemakums*—North of the Twanas were this tribe. In the treaty their name is written Chemakum. Dr. George Gibbs writes it Tsem-a-kum. Hon. J. G. Swan follows the orthography of the treaty, which represents most correctly the way in which both the Indians and the whites of the region pronounce it. The whites call a prairie by the same name. These people call themselves A-hwa-ki-lu, as well as Chemakum.

They formerly occupied the land from the mouth of Hood's Canal to the mouth of Port Discovery Bay. According to their tradition and that of Kwilleutes, they originally came from the latter tribe, (who live on the Pacific coast about thirty miles south of Cape Flattery) and a hundred and twenty-five miles distant, and from whom they are

now separated by the Makahs and Clallams. Hon. J. G. Swan says in regard to this in his work on the Makahs (p. 57.) that the Kwilleutes have a tradition that a long time ago, there was a very high and sudden tide which took four days to ebb, after which a portion of the tribe made their way down to the vicinity of Port Townsend, and are known as Chemakums. The latter have a similar tradition and the numerals of the two tribes corroborate the same.

They are said originally to have been a very warlike tribe, not very numerous, but strong and brave. They had a village near where Irondale or Port Hadlock is now, they called Tsets-i-bus, which is said to have been a kind of capital for nearly all of the tribes on the Sound, and where they occa-

In the 1880's there were no more traditional potlatches on the Sound. In their place celebrations were held on Fourths of July. Here, at Port Hadlock, six miles below Port Townsend, Old Patsy, a Squaxin, held a week-long feast attended by Quillayutes from the Pacific, and Sound peoples — Snohomish, Skokomish, Lummi, Suquamish and Klallams. Canoes are seen here arriving for the event.

Potlatch house at Port Hadlock, used by Old Patsy in 1891 to distribute articles during the Fourth of July celebration.

sionally collected for various purposes. Dr. Gibbs, in 1852, stated their number to have been ninety, but they are now virtually extinct, there being none left who are not married to white men or into other tribes. The last complete families connected themselves with the Clallam Indians, but death has destroyed them as families, leaving only scattered individuals and they use the Clallam language. They say that their diminuition was caused by the smallpox, but probably war had much to do with it, as Dr. Gibbs says that they were engaged with wars with the Makah, Clallam, Twana, Snohomish and Duwamish Indians, by whom their power was broken.

III: *The Clallams*—In the treaty, the name is spelled S'Klallam, but the 's' has been dropped and the 'k' changed to a 'c,' wherever the name is used

except in government reports. Their own name for themselves is Nu-sklaim. Their territory formerly extended from Port Discovery Bay west to the Hoko river near the mouth of the Straits of Fuca. Many other bands of the same tribe lived on the northern side of the Straits in British Columbia. The treaty with them, made at the same time as with the Twanas, expected them to go to the Skokomish reservation, and the government was to furnish the means to move them there. This has never been done; they have never been moved and probably never will be. At present many of them have moved further up the sound to obtain work. The following is a description of their villages.

1. Across the bay, opposite Port Gamble, is quite a village of them named Boston, who earn their money largely at the saw-mills there. Until within a few years, Port Ludlow has had a few, but they are now gone. 2. Near Port Townsend are a few who

make their living by fishing. 3. Opposite Port Discovery, is a small village of those who live mainly by working in the saw-mill there. They have bought the land on which their houses stand. 4. At Sequim, are the last remnants of a band which formerly was of considerable importance. 5. At Jamestown, five miles from Dungeness, is a flourishing village of those who formerly lived at Dungeness and Sequim. It is the most influential village in the whole tribe. They bought land, laid it off into a town and have a school, church and jail. The home of the head chief is here. They gain their living by farming on their land, canoeing, fishing and working for the neighboring whites. Twenty years ago, they were a drunken, worthless set, so that the neighboring whites petitioned the Indian agent to remove them to the Skokomish reservation. Hearing of this, the leading ones, as they did not wish to be removed from the land of their fathers, determined to reform. Gathering together five hundred dollars, they bought two hundred and

ten acres of land, divided it among themselves, according to the amount contributed by each one, and have since that time, been slowly improving. They have also improved in morals, until now they are the most civilized and prosperous band in the tribe. 6. At Port Angeles, has been another village of considerable importance. Many years ago, when the U.S. Custom House was here, work was abundant and the Indian village lively, but as the custom house was washed away, and the business removed to Port Townsend, most of the whites moved away, employment became scarce and nearly all the Indians went away, not to return again, a good share having crossed the Straits to the British side. About a dozen are all that are now left. 7. At Elhwa, was formerly the largest band of the tribe, but they have now largely diminished in numbers and strength. Five or six of them have homesteaded land a mile or two back from the beach, the only ones of the whole tribe who live so far from salt water. These Indians live by canoeing,

The Skokomish Agency (in the background) prior to the twentieth century, located on the flats at the mouth of the Skokomish River.

Potlatch house built on the Skokomish Reservation in 1875. Its dimensions were 40 by 200 feet. Eells' sketch of the inside of this house appears on page 21.

Two views of the Dalles of the Skokomish River,
an important fishing resort for the Indians.

fishing and what they raise on their places, and in the later part of winter and spring, go to the Makah waters for seals. 8. About Pysht are a few families who live mainly by fishing and sealing. 9. At Clallam Bay, about 1880, a number bought about a hundred and fifty acres of land in imitation of their Jamestown neighbors. They did not, however, progress as rapidly, as for many years there were very few whites nearby to encourage and teach them. There were not enough children among them to warrant the establishment of a school and a greater proportion of them were old and non-progressive. They raised a little on their land, fished and hunted seals. About 1891 a boom took place in Clallam Bay. Two towns sprang up, the lands of these Indians became very valuable, and they sold out, to dwindle away.

According to the census of these Indians, which I took for the United States in 1880, they were then distributed as follows:

Six were on or near the Skokomish reservation, ten at Seabeck, ninety-six at Port Gamble, six at Port Ludlow, twelve at Port Townsend, twenty-two at Port Discovery, eighteen at Sequim, one hundred and twenty-two at or near Jamestown, fifty-seven at Port Angeles or across the Straits from that place, sixty-seven at Elhwa, twenty-four at Pysht, forty-six at Clallam Bay and three at Hoko. Since that time, those at Skokomish, Seabeck, Port Ludlow and Hoko have left those places and nearly all have left Sequim and Port Angeles. I can learn of only two dialects which were spoken by this tribe: those at Elhwa, Pysht and Clallam Bay speaking, it is said, as if with thicker tongues than the others, and so pronouncing some words differently.

IV: *The Lummi* — These Indians were situated on the east side of the Sound to the extreme northern part of Washington. They speak another dialect of the Clallam language and for some reasons, ought to be included in the account of that tribe, but owing to their situation, were included in the treaty made with the Snohomish Indians and others in that locality, and hence, have become virtually more distinctly separated from the Clallams than they were before the treaty was made. There were three bands of these, the Lummi, proper, who lived about the mouth of the Nook-sack river; the Swallah, who lived on Orcas and San Juan islands and the Buk-sak, who lived up the Nook-sack river. According to Dr. Gibbs, this latter band spoke a dialect so different from that of the Lummis, as to be almost unintelligible to them.

V: *The Samish* — These Indians lived about the Samish river, south of Lummis. They speak the same language, but are said to be a distinct tribe. There were but two bands of them; the Samish, who lived at the mouth of the river, and the Bis-tla-tlous, who lived up the river.

The Upper and Lower Lilliwaup Falls of the Skokomish River, an Indian fishing place.

Fishing canoes. Eells identified the one on the right as a Haida craft. These canoes, made of one piece of wood with fir rim added, were used for hunting, fishing, and traveling the Sound on calm days.

VI: *Skagits*—This tribe lived south of the Samish Indians, and by language are more nearly related to the Snohomish and Nisqually tribes, on the south, than to their northern neighbors. They lived mainly near the Skagit river. As near as I can learn from the Indians, there were five bands: the Swinomish, who lived on the salt water not far from the mouth of the river, and on Fidalgo Island and on Whidby's Island, opposite; the Do-kwa-tcabsh who lived on the river at the mouth; the Sba-li-hu, who resided farther up, on what might be called the middle of the river; the Sba-le-hu, whose country was on the northern branch which flows from Mt. Baker; and the Sak-wi-be-hu, who lived on the southern branch of the river. Dr. Gibbs also mentions the Kikiallu, Nukwatsamish, Tow-ahha, Sakumehu, Miskaiwhu, Miseekwigweelis and Skwonamish, but does not state whether they are villages or bands, or where they lived.

VII: *The Snohomish*—These lived south of the last named tribe, south of the Stillagwamish river

to the Snohomish river and on both sides of it and its branches. The Indians speak of four bands: the Du-gwads-habsh, who lived on the southern part of Whidby's Island; the Snohomish proper, whose home was near the mouth of the river of that name; the Ske-hwa-mish, on the north fork of the Snohomish River, which on some maps is marked the Skywhamish, and on others the Skykomish; and the Snoqualmie, who lived on the southern branch of the Snohomish river, called the Snoqualmie River. Dr. Gibbs also mentions the Sk-tah-le-jun, Kwehtl-mamish, and Stolutswham-ish bands. While he confirms the statements of the Indians that the Snoqualmie or Snokwalmu band was very intimate with and properly belonged to this tribe, he also says that their dialect of the language agrees more nearly with the Indians on their south, that is, with the Nisqually language proper.

VIII: *The Duwamish*—These lived on the Duwamish river and its tributaries, and on the islands and peninsulas across the Sound, west of the same region. Some of them are on the Port Madison and some on the Muckleshoot reservation. They were divided into several bands, as the Duwamish, Sukwamish, Samamish, Skopahmish, Sk'telmish and St'kahmish.

IX: *Puyallups*—These were formerly called Puyallupahmish and lived on the Puyallup river and Vashon's island opposite its mouth. The Puyallups proper lived about the mouth of the river, the T'kaw-kwa-mish, on its upper branches, and S'ho-ma-mish on Vashon Island. They were formerly not very important, but have of late years become so, because their reservation is the most valuable on the Sound.

X: *The Nisqually, or Squalliamish*—These lived mainly about the Nisqually river, south of the Puyallups and about Olympia and some of the bays west of it. The bands were the Stu-lakumamish, who lived near where Steilacoom now is; the Segwallitsu, the S'hotlemamish, of Case Inlet or North Bay; the Sahehwamish, of

Each fall at hop-picking time Puget Sound Indians were joined by natives from east of the Cascade Mountains, from Vancouver Island, the British Columbia mainland coast, and from as far north as southern Alaska.

Hammersly Inlet, or Skookum Bay; the Sawamish, of Totten Inlet, or Oyster Bay; the Skwaiaitl, of Eld Inlet or Mud Bay; the Stehtsasamish, of Budd Inlet, where Olympia now stands and the Nusehtsatl, of Henderson's Inlet or South Bay. Dr. Gibbs includes the Puyallups with these as one tribe and probably this was correct formerly, but they have now become separated into two tribes owing to reservation system.

XI: *The Squaksons*—East of the Twanas and west of the Puyallups at and around the base of the great peninsula between Hood's Canal and the main Sound, were the Squaksons; or Skwaksnamish. They speak a dialect of the Nisqually language and were included in the treaty with that tribe at Medicine Creek, but owing to their nearness to the Skokomish reservation (about twenty miles) and their intermarriages with the Twanas, their children have been largely brought to the Skokomish reservation to school.

XII: *The Chehalis*—These upper Chehalis Indians live on the upper branches of the Chehalis River as far down as and including the Satsop. Their proper name is not Chehalis; they have given me Kwai-ailk as their name. Dr. Gibbs says

that they are known by the Sound Indians by the name of the Staktamish, by others as the Nu-so-lupsh and by the Willowpah as the Kwu-teh-ai. The Chehalis proper live near the mouth of the Chehalis River, and they thus gave their name to the stream, the whites having first visited it at the coast; after that the Indians on the upper branches became known as the Upper Chehalis Indians. I have not been able to learn that they were divided into bands, but one Indian has given me the names of forty-eight villages, which they once occupied between the Satsop branch and the Cascade mountains. Those below the Satsop are called the Lower Chehalis Indians.

All of these Indians belong to the Salishan family. This family is quite large and includes also the Quinaielts on the west, the Tilamooks and Siletz Indians in Oregon on the south, the Spokanes, Okanogans, Colvilles and Flatheads of Eastern Washington, the Coeur D'Alenes and Pend O'Reilles of northern Idaho, and the Thompson's river, Nanaimo, Cowichan and other tribes in British Columbia to the fifty-third parallel.

These Puget Sound Indians are bounded on the northwest also by the Makahs and Quillyhutes [Kwilleutes, see above] on the southeast by the Cowlitz Indians, and on the east by the Yakamas and Klikitats.

Chief Seattle, whose name was given to the large Puget Sound city was a mixed blood of Suquamish-Duwamish descent. It is said that he never mastered the English language. Although as an infant his head was flattened in the aristocratic manner of his people, the deformity was so slight as to be scarcely noticed. Though Seattle died June 7, 1866, before Eells arrived on the Sound, the missionary collected material about the chief, including this photograph.

COPYRIGHT
1891.

85

A **group of Puyallup** Indian boys at the Indian
Industrial School at Forest Grove.

Eells' History of the Tribes

Their own account of their origin and history.—
They believe that all except the Chemakums were
created where they now live, and also that nearly
all other tribes and nations were created where
they now are. They have hardly any reliable knowledge of their own history earlier than the recollec-
tion of the oldest Indians. Even in obtaining their
names for various articles, I have often found that
persons of twenty or twenty-five years, do not
know their names for stone arrow heads, axes,
chisels, anchors, rain stones and the like, which
went out of use soon after the coming of the whites.
This shows how quickly the past is forgotten by
them.

I give the following stories, in which I presume
there are more or less grains of truth, most of
which were written for me by a Twana school boy,
as they were told him by his father, and which are
about all I have learned from them about their
history.

The Quinaielt and Quilceed Indians.—"While
the Quilceed Indians were at peace in their habita-
tions, a girl went out and looked into a house and
saw (in her mind) many of their enemies getting
ready to go into every house of the Quilceeds. She
returned and told her master's family, but they
would not believe her. The same day a boy went to
get some water; when he looked into the water he
saw some shadows, which were smiling, and these
were the Quinaielt Indians. So he went home in
haste to tell his parents, but they would not believe
him. The girl took one of her master's sons and hid
in the woods. Hence these Indians were not afraid,
and so were all killed except the girl, the little boy,
and one man, for the Quinaielt Indians went into
every house and slew the Quilceeds. One man took
his small babe and ran away. His enemies pursued
him, and when he saw that they were about to
overtake him, he laid down his child and began to
swim across the bay. The Quinaielt Indians knew
that they could not swim after the man, so they
took his child and cut it in pieces. When the girl
came back, she found her master dead, because he
would not believe her."

The Skokomish Indian school in 1893.

The Victoria Indians and Two Families.—"Two families were traveling together and at night they lodged. While they were there someone shot from the woods, and when they looked they saw some Indians. One family went off as fast as it could, but the other had left their child near a log. The Victoria Indians took him, but his father got ready and fired at them, and they restored the child. My father thought that if they should shoot at their enemies, they would think him brave and be afraid. The child that was taken captive is still living, and the daughter of the brave is also alive."

The Quinaielt Indians Again.—"After the battle the Quilceeds went out to search for their enemies, whom at last they found. Then they made a great shelf over their own beds. Their enemies came and were placed under the shelf, and one of them took a wife of the daughters of the Quilceeds. After a long time they laid themselves down on their beds, and the Quilceeds cut the ropes which held up the shelf. It fell down on the heads of the Quinaielt Indians and none of them escaped.

Once the Quilceeds bored some holes in the bottom of their canoes, as their enemies came to see them. As they went home the Quilceeds started to take them across the bay. When they were in the middle of the bay, they took out the sticks, and the water came into the canoes and filled them. The Quinaielt Indians were not drowned because their neighbors went to them and helped them. So the Quilceeds prevailed over their enemies and peace was once more restored."

Story of Another Family.—"There was a man with his wife and children. One woman who was very fair was walking with a babe, and some boys and girls. She was the daughter of a sick man, but when she came home, she found some other Indians killing the family, and her father was killed. These took hold her; one wanted her, another wanted her, and all wanted her; so they killed her and none had her. The man's wife dug deep in the ground, put one of her daughters there, and covered her over; she did also the same for herself, and another person climbed a tree, and none saw her. So three were saved alive. The man was sick, yet they showed him no mercy."

Two Skokomish Indians stand atop springboards. The third man is non-Indian. Besides logging, many Indian men worked in sawmilling, many of them preferring these tasks to farming.

A Fight With a Grizzly Bear. – "A long time ago a man came to the Canal to marry a wife. He found one and gave something to her father. The woman loved the man, but the man did not like his son-in-law, but threw the things away, which the man had given him; hence the man went home. After a while the woman went to gather some berries; my mother's mother was among them. The woman had a companion, and the two went away from their comrades, where they saw the bear, but they did not fear it; they simply talked about it and made fun. The bear went off, but after a time they saw it again, when they talked just as at first. The bear went around the woman who had wished to marry the man, and suddenly jumped at her. The other woman went to help her, but soon received some wounds, so that she left, and went to tell her other comrades, while this woman kept fighting with the bear. Poor woman! She called aloud to her companions to help her, but they ran home to tell the news. She was soon killed; but her friends told her parents, and that night very many people gathered together with spears, arrows and knives to fight the bear. When they reached the place they told the woman's parents to stand on a fallen tree where they would be safe. Then they surrounded the bear and had a great fight; they shot the bear and wounded her on each side, but after a while she ran away, and they ran after her. After a time they had no more arrows or spears, with the exception of two or three young men who still followed her. When they reached a muddy place, she stood on her hind legs and danced; the young men became frightened and ran back. When they looked at the dead woman they found very many wounds on her."

Thus far I have given the stories as they were written for me by a school boy, A. P. Peterson. The last one I presume is in the main true, as I have heard it from several parties.

The Twanas relate that a long time ago they were camped in a scattered condition on Hood's Canal, nearly ten miles south of Seabeck. The Clallams came and killed those furtherest north and took four or five girls captive. Those further south were afraid, and some wished to flee, but others said no. The Clallams however did not come to them, but returned.

Again I add some war stories as written for me by A. P. Peterson. "For some cause the Quilceeds and Skokomish Indians got mad with each other, and got ready for battle. I do not know all about it, but my father tells a part of it. The Quilceeds were in a canoe going home with my mother, whom they took from my father, when my father took his gun, and would have killed all of them, if someone had not taken the gun away from where it was pointing, and it shot off another way. The Quilceeds then went home, and they became friends again."

Thus what was called war ended without any bloodshed.

The following traditions have also been related to me, which may have a few grains of truth in them for a foundation. A long time ago a large number of Indians came up Hood's Canal, and landed near Enetu, on the beach, west of the mouth of the Skokomish river, instead of going up the river, as they were not acquainted with the country. The Twanas were camped on the Skokomish River, about four miles above its mouth. Their enemies intended to surprise them, and so conquer them, but owing to their ignorance of the country, they proceeded to march overland to where the Twanas were camped, and consequently fell into a great swamp, which still exists and is considered impassable. Here they stuck and could not get out, until at last they were stung to death by multitudes of mosquitoes. Tradition also says that long afterwards, some of the Twanas visited the place, and saw the bones, bows, arrows, and spear-heads of their enemies, still there.

The Twanas also say that many years ago, perhaps eighty or a hundred, nearly all the Indians on the Sound leagued together to fight the Indians of British Columbia. This league included the Twanas, Squaksons, Chemakums, Clallams, Snohomish, Puyallup, Nisqually, and Skagit Indians, who went in hundreds of canoes and with thousands of warriors. They intended to surprise their enemies. When near Victoria they however met a large number of the Northern Indians in canoes, but they were many less in number than the Sound Indians. The Sound Indians urged the others to fight, but they did not wish to do so, and only consented after a large amount of urging. The battle continued all day, when the Sound Indians were defeated, with great slaughter, the British Columbia Indians being by far the best fighters. Only a few of the defeated Indians ever lived to return; in some cases only three or four of a tribe. One or two are reported as having escaped by swimming. Having swam for a long time, they reached a floating tree, upon which they remained for nearly a month, without clothes or food, yet they did not perish. At last they drifted to land on the southern side of the Straits and so returned home.

History by the Whites. – Dr. Gibbs in volume one, Contributions to American Ethnology has probably given the most correct history extant of the early visits of the whites to this region, of which I make a short synopsis. The first visit of which we have any knowledge was in 1789, by Captain Kendrick of the American vessel Washington, or in 1790 by Lieutenant Quimper of the Spanish vessel Princess Royal. They came as far as Dungeness. The Indians thought them and their vessel to be

Dokibatl, the great deity of the Puget Sound Indians, as they then knew nothing of the white men. Accordingly when they visited the ship, they painted their faces, and prepared themselves for a tamahnous. Captain Kendrick came as far as the entrance to Admiralty Inlet. Two other vessels came a year and a half later, but they did not come further than Port Discovery Bay.

In 1792 Lord Vancouver came, who gave the first account extant in regard to the Indians. He visited all of the Indians on the Sound, and gave names to the various places, most of which remain to the present time. The people did not seem surprised at his expedition. With one exception they were all quiet and peaceable. Those who showed signs of hostility were "some distance up the first arm leading to the westward above the Narrows" above Vashon Island, evidently among the Squakson Indians, but owning to precaution, all trouble with them was avoided. After these explorers in the early part of the present century the Hudson Bay Company came, and the greater part of the intercourse which these Indians had with the whites, was with that company previous to 1850, though a few Americans came to the Sound in the forties. The Methodist missionaries and Catholic priests came in 1839, the latter to stay, and have missions among the Indians, more especially among the northern tribes. The Hudson Bay Company had one trading post on the Sound, Fort Nisqually, established in 1833, while the one at Victoria, B.C., was so near that many of the northern Indians on the Sound traded there.

After 1850 the influence of Americans began to increase, and that of the Hudson Bay Company to wane with the Indians, and in 1854, the next year after Washington was organized as a Territory, the United States sent Gov. I. I. Stevens, Col. M. C. Simmons, and a few associates to make treaties with them.

December 26, 1854, a treaty was made at Medicine Creek with the Puyallup, Nisqually, and Squakson Indians, together with a few small, associate tribes. By the terms of this, three reservations were set apart for the use of these Indians, the Puyallup reservation, at the mouth of the Puyallup river, the Nisqually reservation, about six miles above the mouth of the Nisqually river, and the Squakson reservation, consisting of the Squakson Island.

The Puyallup reservation now consists of 18,062 acres, and is the most valuable reservation on Puget Sound, as it consists mainly of rich bottom land, adjoining Tacoma, the terminus of the North Pacific Railroad. In 1886 these lands were patented to the Indians in severalty. The school for the benefit of the Indians belonging to this treaty is situated here, their physician and other employes

reside here, and it is now the headquarters for the agent of all the Upper Sound Indians.

The Nisqually reservation consists of 4,717 acres which in 1884 were patented to these Indians in severalty.

The Squakson reservation consists of 1,494 acres, all of which is timbered land, not far above the level of the sea, and a large share of it may be called second class land. In 1884 these lands were patented to these Indians in severalty.

January 22, 1855, at Point Elliot, a treaty was made with the Duwamish, Etakmur, Samish, Skagit, Lummi, Snohomish, Sukwamish, Swinomish and Port Madison Indians. By it, four reservations were set apart for their use. The Tulalip or Snohomish reservation comprises 22,490 acres. Here is the school, the residence of the agent and most of the other employees. In 1885 and 1886 these Indians received patents for their lands — most of which is second quality land.

The Swinomish reservation consists of 7,170 acres. About five hundred acres of this is first quality, tide marsh land. The rest is gravelly and upland, and very poor.

The Lummi reservation lies at the mouth of the Nooksack river, not far from the northern boundary of Washington Territory, and comprises 12,312 acres — for which the Indians received patents in 1884. More than half of this land is very valuable — first quality.

The Port Madison reservation lies on the opposite side of the bay from the town of Port Madison. There are 7,284 acres in it. It is mostly land of a poor quality.

The treaty of Point No Point was made January 26, 1855, with the three tribes of Chemakums, Clallams, and Twanas. By it, but one reservation was set apart for the Indians — the Skokomish consisting of 4,987 acres — three fifths of which is number one bottom land, and the rest is hilly and gravelly. In 1886 these lands were patented to the Indians.

Native cemeteries on the Sound consisted of wooden houses in which bodies were stacked. Some bodies were placed in these houses after being taken from elevated canoe "burials." Some bodies were later buried in the ground. The houses in the picture are like those which Eells sketched.

By orders of the President the Muckleshoot reservation was set apart for the benefit of the Muckleshoot Indians, January 20, 1857, and April 9, 1874. This reservation consists of 3,367 acres, on White River, a branch of the Duwamish, and attached to the Tulalip Agency. This is good bottom land.

An attempt was made by Gov. Stevens in February, 1855, to negotiate a treaty with several tribes of Indians on and adjoining the Chehalis River, consisting of the Cowlitz, Upper Chehalis, Satsop, Lower Chehalis, Chenook, Quinaielts, and Queets, but it was a failure, and consequently no reservation was given them by treaty. By an order from the Secretary of the Interior dated July 8, 1864, the Chehalis reservation was set apart for the benefit of the Upper Chehalis Indians. This consists of 4,225 acres, is situated on the Chehalis River, at the mouth of Black river and is attached to the Nisqually Agency. About one fourth of this reservation is number one bottom land—most of the rest is gravelly, upland, and not good for much except pasture. These lands not being granted by treaty but by order from the President could not be patented to the Indians in severalty as the other reservations were, but were thrown open to settlement about 1886 and were immediately entered as homesteads by the Indians who had the first right to enter them and very soon they proved up and received their patents.

Hostilities.—The first bloodshed on the Sound as far as I can learn was in 1849, at which time an American settler Leander C. Wallace, was killed at Nisqually by the Snoqualmie and Skehwamish Indians. Six of these were soon afterwards taken and tried, two of whom were found guilty and executed.

In 1855 and 1856, soon after the treaties just mentioned were made, but before most of them were ratified, the Yakama war occurred, which was the most widespread Indian war that ever devastated the North Pacific coast. It extended from Southern Oregon, about Rogue river to the Yakamas on the north, and from Puget Sound on the west to the Burnt River and the Grand Rounde Valley in Eastern Oregon. A part of the Indians on Puget Sound were engaged in it, mainly those living around Olympia, Steilacoom, Tacoma and Seattle, namely the Squaksons, Nisquallies, Puyallups, Duwamish and White river Indians. These were led by Leschi, the greatest war chief Puget Sound has produced, a Nisqually Indian, his brother Quiemuth, Kitsap, Nelson and Stehi. The Snohomish Indians led by Patkanim assisted the whites. The other tribes on the Sound did not engage in the war, and people lived among the Twanas in safety during the whole of the time. The

worst massacre was on White river, though the country around Tacoma and Seattle was devastated, to what amount I cannot learn, but in 1886, bills for damages by the people of King County alone, remained unpaid to the amount of $50,666.81. Volunteers were raised, several battles were fought, and the hostiles were driven across the Cascade Mountains. There the leaders were taken. Leschi was convicted and hanged. Quiemuth was assassinated by the son-in-law of Lieutenant J. McAllister, whom he had murdered, and the rest, after trial, were acquitted. Before the war closed a number of Indians from British Columbia came to engage in it. They committed depradations near Steilacoom, and then started to return, but were overtaken by a United States war vessel, under Commander S. Swartout at Port Gamble. The Indians numbered 117 fighting men, and after several offers of peace, if they would leave the Sound, which they rejected, they were attacked and completely conquered, with twenty-seven killed. This was the closing act of the drama on the Sound.

The only act of hostility, which was ever committed on Hood's Canal, as far as I can learn, was by a Clallam Indian, many, many years ago—how long is not known. I have heard the tradition both among the whites and Indians and know of no reason to doubt its truth. The report is that a person named Captain Hood had excited the enmity of this Indian, who followed him closely, yet secretly, in order to take his life. Hood seems to have been aware of this intent, and one night when he encamped on Hood's spit six miles above Seabeck, he stationed two men to guard him. However they all fell asleep, whereupon the Indian stole up and killed him, and fled to the other, the western-side of the canal. A bare place, which the Indian is said to have ascended, in order to look out for possible pursuers, has been pointed out to me by one of the oldest Indians. The Clallams call the name of the place where he was killed, Hwi-a-ne-ta, a corruption they say of the words white man. The name of the murderer was Kwainaks.

It is a common belief among the whites that both Hood's Canal and Hood's Spit, were named because

A few Puget Sound tribes began white men's-style cemeteries in the late 1870's. In the coffins they placed various articles as they had in their earlier native burials.

of this event, but after considerable investigation, and a little newspaper discussion, I think that the spit was named because of this event, but Vancouver in his voyages says that he named Hood's Channel — now changed to canal — in honor of Lord Hood of England, who was never here to be killed.

The treaty with the Nisqually and Puyallup Indians was ratified soon after it was made and proclaimed April 10, 1855, but the other two treaties were not ratified for four years afterwards, that with the Snohomish and confederated bands having been proclaimed April 11, 1859, and that with the Clallam and Skokomish Indians, April 29, 1859. According to these treaties the Indians connected with the treaty of Medicine Creek were to receive $32,500 as annuities in diminishing installments for twenty years, and $3,250.00 more to enable them to move to their reservation; the Indians connected with the treaty of Point No Point, were to receive $60,000.00 as annuities in the same manner, and $6,000.00 to enable them to remove to the reservations; and those connected with the treaty of Point Elliott were to receive $150,000 as annuities, and $15,000 for removal and settlement. According to these treaties all rights to take fish at their accustomed grounds were secured to the Indians and also to erect temporary houses for curing fish; also to hunt and gather berries on unclaimed lands; annuities were not to be taken for debts of individuals; the tribes were to preserve friendly relations, not to make war except in self defense, and not to conceal offenders against the laws of the United States; they were to free all their slaves and not to purchase any more in the future; nor were they to trade outside of the dominion of the United States nor to allow foreign Indians to reside on their reservations. The President reserved the right to remove the Indians whenever their own or the interests of the Territory might require it, to other suitable places in the Territory where he might see fit, on remunerating them for all expenses and improvements abandoned, or at his discretion might cause the whole or a portion of their lands to be surveyed and allotted in severalty to them. The United States was under each treaty to maintain for twenty years a carpenter, blacksmith and necessary shops, a farmer, a physician with necessary medicines, and to support an agricultural and industrial school with proper instructors.

Soon after the ratification of each treaty the United States began to fulfill her part, and, as far as I know, fulfilled it faithfully to the end of the twenty years. Most of the time, until 1882, there were three agents, each one of whom had charge of the Indians represented by one treaty. In 1882 they were all consolidated under one agent, whose headquarters were on the Snohomish reservation, while the Indians were allowed to reside on their several reservations. The next year the agency was divided in two, one agent to have charge of the Snohomish, Swinomish, Lummi, Port Madison and Muckleshoot reservations, with headquarters at the first named one, and the other to have charge of the Puyallup, Nisqually, Chehalis, Squakson and Skokomish reservations, with headquarters on the Puyallup reservation. The principal boarding and industrial schools have been at the Snohomish, Puyallup, Skokomish and Chehalis reservations, with day schools, more or less, at Port Madison, Port Gamble, Jamestown (near Dungeness), and Lummi. After the expiration of the twenty years most of the employes were discharged, except the school employes and the physicians. By special appropriations these have been continued to the present time.

By the terms of the Dawes bill, passed by Congress, and approved February 8, 1887, all Indians who acquire land in any way or have severed their tribal relations become citizens, hence nearly all the Indians on Puget Sound became citizens at that time, the large share of those living off the reservations having obtained land in some way.

Religiously, the Indians belonging to the Snohomish, Port Madison, Muckleshoot, Lummi and Swinomish reservations have been under the teachings of the Catholics for about forty years; the Puyallup, Nisqually and Upper Chehalis Indians have been chiefly under the Presbyterians for twenty or twenty-five years, though the Catholics have given some instructions to the Puyallup and Nisqually Indians, and the Twanas, Clallams and Squaksons have been chiefly under the Congregationalists for twenty years.

When this picture was taken a Skokomish maiden wore clothing not then (about a century ago) in use. Eells had some of the items made by those who remembered the since-discarded clothing. Most other pictures in this Appendix however, show Sound Indians wearing super-neat white people's clothing in contrived surroundings and backdrops popular a century ago for picture making.

Eells' Identification of the Native Flora and Fauna and the Indians' Use Thereof

PLANTS. The following fifty native plants are of practical use, besides cultivated, plants and grass for stock.

Alder. The wood is used for firewood, and for making dishes, plates, paddles, bailers, and masks, for the building of fish traps and rough houses, and the bark is used for medicine and dyeing.

Barberry. The bark is used for medicine and the wood for firewood.

Blackberry. The berry is used for food, the juice for paint, the young leaves for tea, and the juice for medicine.

Cattail rush. The blades are used for making strings, ropes, mats, and one kind of baskets; the mats which are made from them, being one of their most useful articles. The head of this rush was formerly used in making blankets.

Red Cedar. This is the most useful vegetable production of their country. Its wood is used for planks for houses and burial enclosures, for rails, shingles, shakes, posts and the like; also for canoes, oars, baby boards, buoys, spinning wheels, boxes, torches, arrow shafts, fish traps, tamahnous sticks, and firewood; the limbs for baskets and ropes; the bark for baskets, mats, sails, infant head protectors, strings, bailers; and when beaten, for women's skirts, beds for infants, wadding for guns, napkins, head bands, blankets, and for gambling purposes; the gum and leaves for medicine, and the roots for making baskets.

Cherry. The bark is used for strings and medicine.

Cottonwood. The wood is used for firewood, the bark for medicine and strings, and the buds for medicine.

Cranberry. The berry is used for food, the juice for paint, and the young leaves for tea.

Crab-apple. The wood is used for wedges, hoes, mauls, mallets and firewood; the fruit for food and the bark for medicine.

Currant. The berry is occasionally used for food.

Dogwood. The wood is manufactured into gambling disks and hollow rattles, and is used for fuel.

Elder. The wood is made into arrow-heads, which are used as play-things; the bark is used for medicine, and the berry for food.

Fir, red. The wood is valued for firewood, lumber, masts, spear handles, spits and oars; the bark is preferred to everything else for fuel, as it is often three inches, and sometimes six inches thick and pitchy; the pitch wood is good for fire pots, torches and kindling, and for the latter purpose is sometimes sold to the whites; the pitch is used for fastening on arrow and spear-heads, and for cement.

Gooseberry. There are two varieties, both of which are used for food.

Grass — specific name unknown — is used extensively in making and ornamenting baskets. It is found in swamps.

Hazel. The nuts are used as food, the wood for rims to snow shoes, nets and the like, and the bark for strings.

Hemlock. The wood serves for firewood and halibut hooks, the leaves for tea, and the branches for covers in steaming food.

Huckleberry, black, blue and red. The berries of all varieties are used for food, and the juice occasionally for paint.

Ironwood. The wood is used for arrow-shafts, arrow and spear-heads, and mat needles, and the bark for medicine.

Indian Onion. The bulb is eaten.

Kelp. Strings and ropes, especially fish-lines are made from the root.

Kamass. The root is edible.

Laurel. The wood is used in making spoons, vessels and fancy articles; the leaves for medicine.

Liquorice. The root is medicinal.

Maple. The wood is useful for hacklers, mat blocks, paddles, oars, bobbins, seine blocks, combs, fish and duck spear-heads, fish clubs, rails and firewood. The leaves are used in steaming. A smaller variety of maple is also used for firewood.

Moss is used to wrap around wood while steaming it to make bows and the like, the whole being buried in the ground.

This native woman wears a mat coat of cattail rushes over a dress made of mountain goat wool. She wears a gorget of dentalia shells.

NETTLES. The fiber is used in making strings, a twine, the strongest they had.

Oregon Grape. The root and bark are valuable as a medicine, and the root for dyeing yellow.

Peuce-da-num. The stem is used for food, and the seeds, when ripe, as a medicine, being peppery.

Raspberry. The berry is used for food, and the juice as a paint.

Rose. The root and leaves are a medicine.

Rush. A round kind of rush is used in making mats.

Sallalberry. The berry is used for food.

Salmonberry. The berry and young shoots are eaten.

Skunk Cabbage. The leaves are used for medicine, and the roots occasionally for food.

Strawberry. The berry serves as food.

Thimble Cap. The berry and young shoots are eaten.

Spruce. The wood is burned, and is also carved; the roots are used in making halibut hooks, and the leaves serve as medicine.

Vine Maple. The wood is burned for fuel.

Willow. The bark is used for strings, and the wood occasionally for fuel.

Yew. Paddles, bows, arrows, and fish clubs of the best kind are made of the wood.

Fern. The roots beaten, were formerly used as food.

Kinnikinnick. The berry is used for food, and the leaves dried, are occasionally mixed with tobacco for smoking when the latter article is scarce.

Fireweed. The cotton-like down from the seed was formerly used in making blankets.

Plants not identified. The roots of two varieties, the tops of one of them, and the root of another variety is eaten. One of them is a rush, the equiselum.

BEASTS. The following seventeen kinds are useful to them.

Bear — black. The flesh is eaten, the skin is used for robes and arrow quivers, and is sold to the whites.

Bear — grizzly. Though scarce, its skin was used for robes, and the Indians believed it to be a very strong tamahnous animal, which was supposed to be used by the medicine men in making people sick.

Beaver. The meat is good for food, the skin for furs, and the teeth are used in the women's games of gambling.

Cat-wild. The flesh was occasionally eaten, and the skins were used for robes. It was also a tamahnous animal.

Dog, common, is of use for hunting, domestic purposes, and the like.

Dog — wool. The hair was used for making blankets. The breed is now extinct.

Deer. This is probably the most useful wild animal known to them. The flesh is used for food, the skins for robes, strings, fringes, moccasons, clothes, shot-pouches and the like; the fawn skins are sometimes made into buoys for whaling; formerly they made shirts which answered the purposes of shields or suits of armor from the skins; the sinews they use for thread, the hoofs for rattles in religious dance, and the brains in tanning.

Elk. The flesh serves for food, the skins for robes and shield-shirts, and when dressed for strings and clothes, and of the horns they make wedges, chisels and paint. The animal is in most respects used much as the deer, but is not so common by far.

Mink. The skins are useful as furs.

Muskrats. The skins are useful as furs and the teeth in gambling occasionally.

Otter. The flesh is eaten.

Otter, sea. The skins are among the most valuable furs.

Panther. The skins are made into robes and clothes. It is also a tamahnous animal.

Raccoon. The skin is used for furs and the flesh for food.

Sheep or Goat — Mountain. The flesh is used as food and the horns for dishes and ladles.

Wolf. The skin is used for robes, quivers and caps. It is likewise a tamahnous animal.

The intestines of several of these animals are used for holding oil, and the bones for various articles, as awls, arrow and spear heads, combs, fasteners and the like.

Birds. —There are seventeen kinds which they utilize as follows: The crane, seven varieties of ducks, i.e. the mallard, pin-tail, wood-duck, scoter, teal, diver, and canvas back, the grouse, goose, two varieties of loons, and the pheasant are used as food, while the feathers serve as beds, pillows, and ornamenting the hair at festivals. The Gull also occasionally serves for food for old people, and the feathers for beds, though they are rather coarse.

John Haiten, a Nisqualli Indian, with ceremonial shirt of deer skin and tamanous articles in his hands.

Eagle-hawk, and red-headed woodpecker. The feathers are useful for feathering arrows, and in tamahnous head-bands.

Kingfisher. A piece of the skin where the tail or wing feathers enter it was formerly used in fishing, attached to the line near the hook, as it was superstitiously supposed that it would attract the fish.

Fish and other marine animals.—Thirty-six kinds of these are used by them. The following are eaten: Three varieties of clams, two of crabs, two of codfish, and their eggs, the dog-fish when food is very scarce, two kinds of flounders, the halibut, herring, muscles, oyster, porpoise, five varieties of salmon with their eggs, namely, silver, red, dog, black and hump-backed, the hair seal occasionally, smelt, sea eggs, scallop, skate, sturgeon, trout, whale, cuttle-fish, and one called *tse-kwuts* by the Twanas.

The shells of the abalone, dentalia, and occasionally the olivella, were used as money and ornaments.

Large clam shells were of use as drinking dishes.

The skin of the dog-fish is used as sand paper.

The dog-fish, porpoise, hair-seal, shark and whale furnish valuable oil, some of which is eaten, some used in painting, and some sold to the whites.

From the skin of the hair seal are made buoys used in sealing and hunting, small sacks, hunting pouches, and the like.

Scallop shells are used as rattles in tamahnous.

From the bones of the whale, war clubs and a part of codfish hooks are made, and its sinew is used as thread.

In this posed picture the Twana women wears a woolen garment of native manufacture such as those worn when Captain George Vancouver visited the Sound in 1972. The headpiece is made of dentalium shells.

Some Observations of Eells of the Indians

In the opening pages of his notebooks, Eells wrote of the Indians of Puget Sound: "I should say of the greater part of those under forty-five years of age, at the present time, that if they had white skins, talked the English language, if all of them had abandoned their belief in their medicine men, if they travelled in boats instead of canoes, if the women wore hats or bonnets on their heads, and if they were neat, they would be called civilized, at least as much as the lower classes of whites." He continued: "Generally they are quite industrious, and a trip over most reservations on pleasant days shows that most of the men are at work [often performing the tasks of white men]: on rainy days it is different, as they have but little indoor work to perform. The women however are generally busy, rain or shine, as they can make mats and baskets, when not otherwise busy."

Observing the Indians whether on or off the reservation, Eells noted that they had an amalgam of various blood. Twanas had married into practically every native group of the region, and the Klallams, nearly so, with the blood of eighteen other peoples flowing in their veins. Of all the groups

The color of the eyes and hair is black. As to blushing they are similar to white people, but not so sensitive; as to muscular strength and speed, they are inferior to white people; but in regard to climbing they are superior; their growth is attained early in life, and their decay also begins early; their child bearing is generally very easy, though there are occasional exceptions, which have increased as they become civilized, and some deaths in child birth have occurred; their reproductive power is less than whites; sterility prevails considerably, caused in early life by various kinds of abuse; the age of puberty in males is about fourteen, and with females not far from thirteen; they cross with all races, there being some children who are half Indian and half negro, and a few who are half Indian and half Chinese; their teeth come about the same as with white children, but wear down early in life, and the more they are civilized, owing probably to the sugar and syrup which they eat, the more they decay. Their length of life is probably ten years less than with whites...

He found very few among them either gray or even partially bald, and very few deformed. He knew of three Klallams who had been humpbacked, but two of them had died in childhood, and in his many years among them, of but two cases of insanity — one a Klallam and the other, a Twana. He was constantly aware of their great powers of endurance whether paddling their canoes or suffering myriads of fleas "which would torment a white man beyond endurance." Yet, disease had made its inroads among them. Principal ones were

scrofula, scrofulous swellings and abcesses, all of which are grafted on a scrofulous diathesis, consumption and bleeding of the lungs. They are also largely troubled with acute and chronic bronchitis, catarrh, diarrhea, dyspepsia, conjunctivitis, skin disease, syphilis, gonorrhea, toothache, and chronic rheumatism. Their diet, habits, and the climate have produced a scrofulous diathesis from generation to generation, thus shortening their lives. The dankness of the climate also produces rheumatism and consumption...

He noted eight languages spoken by "these Indians to a greater or less degree, the Twana, Nisqually, with its special dialects of the Snohomish, the Klallam, with its dialect of the Lummi, Chemakum, Upper Chehalis, Lower Chehalis, Chinook Jargon, and English:"

Nearly all of the Indians under thirty-five years old, and the men under forty, — among the Twanas, Puyallups, Port Madisons, Clallams, Chehalis, and Snohomish Indians can talk English, so as to be understood in ordinary conversation, — as well as many over that age, — in fact one half of all the Indians on the Sound. A large number of others

Mr. and Mrs. Charles Jackson, a Klallam family. By Eells' time, most tribes no longer practiced polygamy.

understand simple sentences in it, who cannot easily converse in it. The men understand it better than the women, as they have worked more among white men, who did not talk Chinook Jargon to them, than the women. Those who have never been in school, however, dislike to talk it, far more than they do the Chinook Jargon, because they fear they will not pronounce the words aright, and therefore that someone will laugh at them. Hence they will not speak it, if the person with whom they are talking can talk Chinook Jargon.

Eells believed that among the Indians who had made considerable progress in learning the English language, were the Puyallups, who had even done some printing, the first among the Indians to do so. One of their men in 1879 was setting type on a Tacoma newspaper and another, at the Industrial Training School at Forest Grove, Oregon. Puyallup boys took the lead in putting out a small newspaper at that school with help from boys of other tribes. On their own reservation Puyallup school children had done considerable printing. Snohomish children published a magazine, *The Youth's Companion*, from 1881 to 1886. On all reservations, the missionary believed children had written many letters which they sent through the mails. Some also read newspapers, and one Skokomish Reservation Indian, John Palmer, who died in 1881, had subscribed to five newspapers and magazines. Klallams had also subscribed to various publications.

Eells did not decry traditional beliefs. Instead, he objectively noted many of them: the wind, caused by the breath of a great being; the cold, caused by getting further from the sun in winter; eclipses, caused by whales eating the sun; no laughing at old men or stealing women in day times; no saying of "naughty words" at play; no sitting on rocks so as not to grow fat; no pointing to rainbows lest fingers become sore; no permitting old persons to carry water; and no laughing at them.

As Eells observed it, their numerical system went by tens, and they divided the year into moons, or lunar months, and months into days. This type of reckoning, he believed to have been implemented by finer measures of time with the coming of clocks and in some cases, watches. The old Indian name for days, months, and heavenly bodies, were nearly obsolete, he wrote, young men hardly knowing them at all. Formerly they had names for the seasons. He believed they first obtained the concept of Sundays from Klickitats, after which they often met on that day to talk, pray, dance, and attempt to purify themselves, "to throw away their bad, and name their hearts good." On that day they also married.

Wrote the missionary: "Most old settlers among the Twanas and Clallams, with whom I have conversed, estimate that thirty-five years ago there were from two and a half to five times as many of these Indians as there are now." He believed intemperance decreased after "good" Indian agents were appointed under President Grant, but after Indians became citizens, with acceptance of provisions of the Dawes Severalty Act of 1887, "liberty [had] become with many license, and intemperance [had] increased." In different localities, he though the "vices of unchastity and intemperance [abounded] more than others owing to different causes, but chiefly to their [the Indians'] proximity to towns and cities." A case in point were the Klallams whose close association with unprincipled whites exposed them to drink. He thought a little exaggerated, however, the statement of Klallam chief, Lord Jim Balch, that "the saloons of Dungeness had killed five hundred Clallams in twenty years."

"Their emotions and passions are often very strong," he wrote, "though generally not as lasting as whites." He thought their "moral ideas" quite low formerly, "especially in regard to theft, lying, murder, intemperance, and chastity." But he believed the moral level was rising: "Formerly they would say it was wrong to steal, but if not found out it was apparently all right. Now there are very few who are ever accused of stealing, and murders have of late become almost unknown." "Lying," he went on, "is much more common...In regard to chastity they have improved much, but there is room for improvement."

He found nothing which might have been called a "caste" system among them, unless, as he stated, "the slaves were such." Slavery, he noted, once existing all over the Sound, had just about died out, due, he believed, to an article in the treaties with the government which mandated its abolition. One Twana, however, had three slaves which remained with their master by their own choice.

Besides slaves, most of which he noted were taken in war, there were other classes which he

The David Hunters standing and the Henry Johnsons seated with their children — all dressed in fancy white style clothing. Both families were Klallams. White influences on such families had been so great by the twentieth century as to obscure and eradicate many native customs and habits.

identified as "chiefs, sub-chiefs, head-men, medicine men and women and common people." The status of women in the family and in society he thought inferior to that of white women, "although by no means do they become as near like slaves, as some Indian women in the interior of the continent, are reported to be." As to marriage, he wrote that "when a young man formerly went around picking flowers and carrying them along, it is said that it was a sign that he wished to get married." But Eells also knew that it took more than flowers for matrimony, because "money and property have purchased many a wife on Puget Sound." Divorce he saw as common as very few men or women "went through life without one or more divorces, nor did it lower their social standing. If a man put away his wife, he generally gave her a present, but if she left him, he did not give her anything." Polygamy was permitted, and was common among the more important Indians, but Eells noted that hardly any of it remained. Of polygamy: "I have never known any man to have more than three wives, and any more plural marriages, but at last about 1885 there came an order for all who had more than one wife to put away all but one. In two cases on the Skokomish reservation it required some locking up of some of the parties concerned to enforce this, but it was at last accomplished."

Eells never knew of infanticides except in the case of twins, but abortion was still practiced "more commonly it is said by some medicine they have." Among Klallams formerly as well as in Eells' time pubertal dances were held, although he found no similar practice among Twanas since he had been amongst them. Sexual intercourse among unmarried girls, he noted, brought no disgrace if unaccompanied by childbirth. The practices had disappeared of secluding women as unclean (at the menses) for about a week when they were not permitted to touch fish, flesh, fowl or game, guns and fishing apparatus for fear they would bring bad luck. He wrote that when a woman gave birth to a child she sometimes attended herself, but was generally assisted by some of her female friends, some of these becoming famous midwives and superior in this respect to common women "In a few instances," wrote Eells, "I have known it (childbirth) to cause the death of the mother, and also of the child, though this is not common." He thought that as the people became more "civilized," womens' labor at birth had become more difficult. Children were often nursed until much older than were white children — sometimes until their third year or perhaps later. They also were not named as early as were white children, but were named from one to three years of age. He was unable to learn that their names had meanings, but did know that they no longer held name-giving feasts. He also learned that besides Indian names, they had gotten "Boston" names in various ways:

Some were combination Indian and American names constructed utterly regardless of taste, as Squakson Bill, Old Shell, Mr. Axe, Mr. Stone, Stuttering Dick...Others aim a little higher, but just high enough to make them ridiculous, as Dr. Bob, Mrs. Bob and Sally Bob...Others still have aspired to as great names as America or Great Britain could give. Such as General Grant, Horace Greely, Benjamin Butler, Robert Burns, Patrick Henry and Andrew Johnson. We have had on the Skokomish reservation, both Simon Peter, and Andrew Peter his brother, not sons of Zebidee, but old Peter himself. I once stood at a grave yard at Port Townsend, at the head of a row of graves with an Indian, who rather surprised me by saying 'Here lies General Scott, General Gaines, and General Taylor.' The man, who for many years was the prominent head chief of the Clallams rejoiced in the name of Duke of York, and for those of his two wives, Jenny Lind, and Queen Victoria. I had the honor of performing the marriage ceremony of his son, the Prince of Wales, and to find that on account of his name, that it was telegraphed all over the world among the Associated Press dispatches...The successor of the Duke of York was Lord Jim Balch, but his successor was only Cook House Billy. We have had Duke William, Duke of Wellington, and Lord John whose son was curiously named John Lord.

These old English royal names, were given, when the Hudson's Bay Company held sway here. Afterwards when loggers and mill men settled in the region, who were known to the Indians, and often to many whites only by the names of Jack, John, Pat...The Indians were satisfied when they obtained similar ones. Often so many obtained the same name that some other one, descriptive had to be joined with it, so that we have had Little Billy [,] Big Bill, Sore Eyed Bill and Squakson Bill...Of late years however I have made it my practice, when it could be done, when I legally married the older ones, or they obtained their first legal papers, or when the children enter school, to give them such names that they would not be ashamed of them.

Myron Eells had made in 1892 this "sample of the old dwelling houses" for shipment to the World's Columbian Exposition in Chicago. One-family dwellings of this type with flat roofs were constructed of both upright and horizontal plank boards and used mostly before white men came to Puget Sound. None were inhabited when the missionary had this house built for display.

Where once the practice of head flattening was "universal" Eells found very few infants who had their heads thus misshapened, noting that school teachers on the Skokomish had been unable to detect differences in intellect between those who did and those who did not have their heads so treated. Some Indians, Eells observed, believed the practice to have caused numerous headaches among them in later life.

He thought Indian children did as well as white children in primary school lessons, but as a general rule, not as well as in the more advanced ones. He thought their memories superior to those of white children, but their "reasoning powers" much poorer, although at times reasoning "very sharply." "The strength of will," he wrote, "among a few is quite great, and these become leaders, but the common people have not much."

As he traced changes in the natives' characteristics he also noted those of an institutional nature. Where formerly there had been village autonomy under chiefs exercising little influence away from their villages, their governmental systems had undergone considerable change with the advent of the reservation system:

The influence of the whites had been so great upon Indian customs, that it is about as difficult to discover accurately their ancient habits in regard to government, as in regard to any other customs. In reference to other customs, the moral influence of the whites had its effect, only so far as the Indians were willing to adopt our habits, and enough of the old has remained to help me to trace back the customs to the time when they had only their old habits. But in regard to this branch, the United States Government has stepped in with its Agents, soldiers and power, and has said 'You shall and you shall not do so and so,' until almost every vestige of ancient government is deeply buried in the past.

As the missionary saw it, agents, such as his brother, Edwin, had almost supreme authority over Indians, acting as a supreme court when the latter could not settle their own cases. Agents often made and unmade chiefs. These agents found it impractical, he noted, to immediately abolish gambling and tamanous practices until a respectable minority of the people approved these changes. Among Twanas and Klallams, he recorded that the office of chief was elective [and actually appointive too] and remained during good behavior or until the chief resigned. He thought there were two difficulties with this system: one, that these leaders so installed decided in court in favor of the rich and most numerous; and the other, that sometimes worthless persons were elected to the position. To obviate this, the government appointed paid judges having more government

backing and more independence of the people. Judges also held office until Indians became citizens; then judgeships were abolished. There then remained on the reservation only the Indian policemen who had little power other than that of seeing to it that the children went to school.

Trial and punishment formerly had been "life for a life" in cases of murder, with money and property generally accepted instead, with ample time given a murderer and his friends to give to the victim's family before the murderer's life was taken. Under the rule of agents and judges, however, Eells noted that imprisonment and fines had been the common modes of punishment. Usually a week's imprisonment or a twenty-dollar fine were heavy, but in some instances, sentences of six months in jail were meted out. One Twana, turned over to military authorities at Port Townsend, was confined to six months of hard labor. Largest numbers of violations were for "drunkenness, debts, immoralities, with a few cases of theft." Of debts:

When they can get into debt to a white person, they generally seem to be glad to do so even when they have the money with which to pay, and they keep going into debt often, even though there is no probability of their ever being able to pay, if they are allowed to do so. Unless asked to pay, they seldom offer to do so, unless they are obliged to pay in order to get more, as at a store. Still if pressed a little they generally are willing to make effort to pay ... I once thought that this disposition of the Indians to get into debt to Whites was evidently a race prejudice, as if all they could get from the Whites was clear gain. But the more I have learned of their habits, the more I believe this is not the real cause. That lies in their native training from infancy. They are generally in debt to each other, and these debts are often of very long standing, ten years or more.

Throughout his notes Eells expressed no jeremiads over the Indian condition as had some. Instead, he set out to help them make the transition to Christianity and "full civilization" with no illusions that such states in themselves were utopian.

Peter C. Stanup, a Puyallup Indian, born about 1857, became a typesetter for the Tacoma *Herald.* Wanting to better his education, he was among the first to attend the Indian Industrial School at Forest Grove, Oregon, after which he prepared for the ministry. Although financially successful in real estate operations, he succumbed to liquor and drowned in the Puyallup River in 1893.

A Partial Indian Pharmacopoeia Compiled by Eells

Alder buds. They [natives] eat them, and afterwards drink salt water as an emetic in cases of cold and biliousness.

Alder bark. This they grind in water, and drink the infusion as a tonic.

Barberry bark is prepared in the same way as the last, and used to purify the blood.

Blackberry root is used for colds.

Cedar gum is chewed for toothache.

Cedar leaves are chewed and bound on cuts.

Cherry bark prepared as alder bark for a physic and tonic.

Cottonwood bark, thick from the body of the large trees, after having been soaked in salt water, is ground and used as a medicine.

Cottonwood buds are also used as a medicine.

Crab-apple bark. A cold tea is made from this as a wash for the eyes.

Elder bark. An infusion taken internally and in a vapor bath is used for diarrhea.

Licorice. Used for colds and as a tea for gonorrhea.

Oregon grape. The root and bark are used in the same way as alder bark for skin diseases [and] as a tonic and for venereal.

Rose bark and roots, used for as a medicine.

Potatoes, scraped, for burns and scalds.

Skunk cabbage leaves. They heat rocks, throw water over them, place leaves on them, and get over the steam for strengthening general debility.

Earth is sometimes bound on bruises.

Cautery. Rheumatism is sometimes treated by taking a red-hot iron, or a stick, or small bunch of cedar bark or rag, twisted into the shape of a stick, setting fire thereto and burning a hole in the flesh to the bone. I have seen one Clallam, who had dozens of scars on him from this mode of treatment.

Blood letting is done by scarifying the body in various places.

Soap and sugar are applied as a salve for boils.

A decoction of the white flowering or poisonous kamass furnishes an emetic.

Cucumber vine. A decoction, is used as an emetic and cathartic.

Skunk wood. The inside bark, chewed up, serves as a poultice.

Colt's foot. The juice is used as a fomentation for bruises and sprains.

Hemlock-spruce. Women during their periods of menstruation bind the twigs around their bodies, perhaps as a species of charm. They are also used as a bed for the sick.

For gonorrhea, the females smoke themselves over a fire made of certain plants or wood.

Swelling produced by injuries they sometimes scarify.

Sores that are slow in healing they sometimes cauterize. They employ moxa by the application of coals of fire, and the powder left by worms under the bark of trees is also strewn over them to dry them up. This and potter's clay, dried and powdered, is used for chancres. Suction by the mouth is a remedy to alleviate pain.

Tillie Atkins, a Chehalis woman, whose generation bridged the gap from flea-infested, (to the whites) foul-smelling lodges, to conditions emulating those prevailing among the whites.

A Twana Indian, Joseph M. Spar. As with others
of his tribe, the acculturation process had endowed
him with a white mans' name.

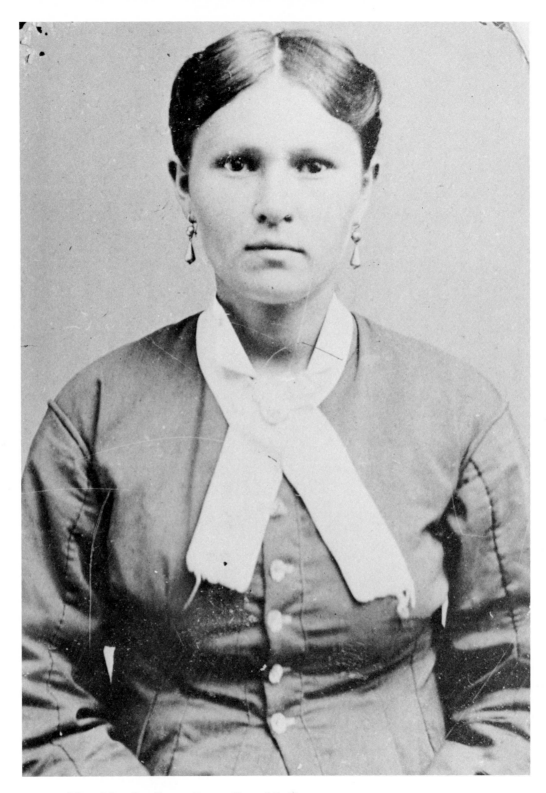

Mrs. Martha Spar. Puget Sound Indian women,
although influenced by white civilization, re-
sponded to it more slowly than did their men.

A Twana woman, Mrs. Mary Adams. Eells noted the status of native women as inferior to that of white women in their society.

John Palmer, born near Port Townsend about 1847, belonged to the now extinct Chemakum tribe. His family died when he was young. He learned to speak English, Russian, and four native Indian tongues, enabling him to serve as an interpreter on several area reservations until his death in 1881.

A Twana woman of one-half white blood. The Strait of Juan de Fuca and Puget Sound in a sense facilitated white settlement along their shores, thrusting the two races together to form such racial amalgams.

George Bridges, a half-blood Klallam of twenty-six years when this picture was taken.

117

Louis Amor, half-Klallam and half-Italian. Children of unmarried white-Indian parents were as numerous as were those of married parents.

A full-blood Twana. From Eells' notes it would appear that few such full-blooded Indians existed in his day.

A Twana man, Milton Fisher. By Eells' time
nearly all Sound tribes wore western dress, although not as neatly as worn by this man for the
camera.

SUGGESTED READING

A partial list of Myron Eells' publications

ARTICLES

(By Eells continued)

"Aboriginal Geographic Names in the State of Washington," *American Anthropologist,* V, 1 (Old Series) January, 1892.

"Washington Territory: Three Indian Boys and Their Letters." *The American Missionary*, XXXII, 4 April, 1878.

"Busy Day of an Indian Missionary," *The American Missionary*, L, 3 March, 1896.

"Catholic Missions—Recent Changes," *The American Missionary*, XXXVII, 7 July, 1883.

"The Chinook Jargon," *American Anthropologist*, VII, 3 (Old Series) July, 1894.

"Church and Sabbath-school Work at S'kokomish, W. T.," *The American Missionary*, XXXVII, 3 March, 1883.

"The dark day in Washington," *Monthly Weather Review*, XXX, 9 September, 1902.

"Decrease of Population Among the Indians of Puget Sound," *American Antiquarian*, IX, 4 September, 1887.

"The Decrease of the Indians," *American Antiquarian*, XXV, 3 May, 1903.

"Dr. Whitman. Another Contribution to the Discussion Respecting Him," *Oregonian*. Portland, Oregon, January 11, 1885.

"Dr. Whitman. Reply to Honorable Elwood Evans," *Oregonian*. Portland, Oregon, February 8, 1885.

"Do-ki-batt; or; the God of the Puget Sound Indians," *American Antiquarian*, VI, 6 November, 1884.

"The First Book Written in the State of Washington," *The Washington Historian*, I, 4, July, 1900.

"Honorable Record for Indians," *The American Missionary,* IL, 2 February, 1895.

"How Languages Grow," *Advance*, March 25 and July 8, 1875.

"Indian Music," *American Antiquarian*, I, 4 April, 1879.

"The Indians of Puget Sound," *American Antiquarian*, IX, 1 January, 1887.

"Indians of Puget Sound," *American Antiquarian*, X, 3 May, 1888.

"Indian War History Errors," *Oregon Native Son*, II, 3 July, 1900.

"The Late Indian War and Christianity," *The American Missionary*, XXXIII, 1 January, 1879.

"New Church at Dunginess," *The American Missionary,* XXXVI, 7 July, 1882.

"One Soweth and Another Reapeth," *The American Missionary*, ILVII, 1 January, 1893.

"The Potlatches of Puget Sound," *The American Missionary*, V, 2 April, 1883.

"Puget Sound Indians," *American Antiquarian,* X, 1 January, 1888.

"The Puget Sound Indians," *American Antiquarian*, IX, 4 July, 1887.

"The Religion of the Clallam and Twana Indians," *American Antiquarian*, II, 1 July, 1879.

"The Religion of the Indians of Puget Sound," *American Antiquarian*, XII, 2 March, 1890.

"Religious Interest at S'kokomish," *The American Missionary*, XXVII, 11 November, 1882.

"A Reply to Professor Bourne's 'The Whitman Legend,'" *Whitman College Quarterly*, IV, 3 October, 1902.

"Report of S'kokomish, Wash." *The American Missionary*, ILVIII, 9 September, 1894.

"Rev. Samuel Parker," *Whitman College Quarterly,* II, 3 October, 1898.

"School and Church Work at Dunginess," *The American Missionary*, XXXIII, 4 April, 1879.

"Shaking Religion," *The American Missionary*, ILVI, 5 May, 1892.

"The Spice of Missionary Life," *The American Missionary,* XXXIII, 6 June, 1879.

"S'kokomish Agency-field and work," *The American Missionary*, XXXIV, 10 October, 1880.

"S'kokomish Agency, Wash.," *The American Missionary,* ILVIII, 4 April, 1894.

"S'kokomish Agency, W. T.," *The American Missionary,* XXXVIII, 5 May, 1884.

"S'kokomish Agency, W.T. Sunday-school Progress—An Indian Festival—Temperance and Order," *The American Missionary*, XXXII, 5 May, 1878.

"S'kokomish Mission, Washington," *The American Missionary*, ILV, 4 April, 1891.

"S'kokomish, Washington Territory," *The American Missionary*, XXXIV, 7 July, 1880.

"The Stone Age of Oregon," *Annual Report of the Board of Regents of the Smithsonian Institution, for 1886*, (49 Cong., 2d sess., Mis. Doc. 170, pt 1, House Doc.), Serial 2498 Washington, 1889.

"Superstitions Among Christian Indians," *The American Missionary*, ILVII, 1 January, 1893.

"Teachers' Institute Among the Indians," *The American Missionary*, ILVII, 1 January, 1893.

"The Thunder Bird," *American Anthropologist*, II, 4 (Old Series) October, 1889.

"A Tour Among the Clallam Indians," *The American Missionary*, XXXIII, 11 November, 1879.

"Traditions and History of the Puget Sound Indians," *American Antiquarian*, IX, 2 March, 1887.

"Trials and Heroism of the Pioneer Women," *Proceedings of the Washington Pioneer Association for the year 1903-1904*, Seattle, 1904.

"The Twana, Chemakum, and Klallam Indians, of Washington Territory," *Annual Report of the Board of Regents of the Smithsonian Institution, for 1887*, (50 Cong., 1 sess., Mis. Doc. 600, pt 1, House Doc.), Serial 2581 Washington, 1889.

"The Twana Indians of the Skokomish Reservation in Washington Territory," *Bulletin of the U.S. Geological and Geographical Survey*, III, 1 Washington, 1877.

"The Twana Language of Washington Territory," *American Antiquarian*, III, 4 July, 1881.

"Variety in Missionary Life," *The American Missionary*, XXXVI, 9 September, 1882.

"Work on a Short Tour," *The American Missionary*, XXXV, 10 October, 1881.

"The Worship and Traditions of the Aborigines of America; or, Their Testimony to the Religion of the Bible," *Victoria Institute, London, Journal of Transactions*, XIX, London, 1885.

BOOKS AND PAMPHLETS
(By Eells)

Address at the Skokomish church (at the funeral of Mrs. Myra F. Eells) Delivered by the youngest son of the deceased, Rev. Myron Eells...Aug. 11, 1878. Portland, 1878.

The collected writings of Myron Eells. Portland, n.d.

The Congregational Church of Forest Grove, Oregon, 1859-1901. Shelton, Wash., 1901.

The Duties of Parents to Baptized Children. Boston, 1885.

Father Eells: A Sketch, 1810-1893. Walla Walla, n.d.

Father Eells; or, The results of fifty-five years of missionary labors in Washington and Oregon. Boston, 1894.

Funeral Services in Memory of Mrs. M. F. Ells (sic), One of the Pioneer Missionaries of the A.B.C.F.M. to the Spokane Indians of Oregon, in 1838, Snohomish and Seattle, W.T., August 11 and 13, 1878.

The hand of God in the history of the Pacific coast: Annual address delivered before the trustees, faculty, students, and friends of Whitman college at the sixth commencement, June 1, 1888. Walla Walla (?), 1888.

Hymns in the Chinook Jargon Language. Portland, 1878.

The history of Hood canal, Mason county, its discovery, n.p., n.d.

History of Indian missions on the Pacific coast: Oregon, Washington, and Idaho. Philadelphia, 1882.

History of the Congregational association of Oregon, and Washington territory; the Home missionary society of Oregon and adjoining territories; and the Northwestern association of Congregational ministers. Portland, 1881.

In Memoriam. Rev. S. H. Marsh, D. D., First President of Pacific University, Born August 29, 1825, Died Feb. 2, 1879. Portland, 1881.

Justice to the Indian. Read before the Congregational association of Oregon and Washington, July 14, 1883. n.p., n.d.

Marcus Whitman, M.D.; Proofs of his work in saving Oregon to the United States, and in promoting the immigration of 1843. Portland, 1883.

Marcus Whitman, Pathfinder and Patriot. Seattle, 1909.

Memorial of Mrs. Mary R. Walker, n.p., 1898.(?)

The relations of the Congregational colleges to the Congregational churches. New York, 1889.

A Reply to Professor Bourne's "The Whitman Legend." Walla Walla, 1902.

Ten Years of Missionary Work Among the Indians at Skokomish, Washington Territory, 1874-1884. Boston, 1886.

A Trip from Walla Walla to Tshimakain Near the Spokane river and Return. Seattle, n.d.

MANUSCRIPTS
(By Eells)

Words, Phrases, and Sentences in the Chemakum language, in the library of the Bureau of Ethnology.

Words, Phrases, and Sentences in the S'klallam or Sclallam language, in the library of the Bureau of Ethnology.

Words, Phrases, and Sentences in the Skwaksin Dialect of the Niskwalli Language, in the library of the Bureau of Ethnology.

Words, Phrases, and Sentences in the Twana Language, in the library of the Bureau of Ethnology.

Index